ROMANS

दिनलिपि

Daniel J. Harrington

ROMANS

The Good News
According to Paul

New City Press

Published in the United States by New City Press
202 Cardinal Rd., Hyde Park, NY 12538
©1998 Daniel J. Harrington

Cover design by Nick Cianfarani
Cover art: "The Risen Christ" by Ave Cerquetti

Library of Congress Cataloging-in-Publication Data:
Harrington, Daniel J.
    Romans : the good news according to Paul / Daniel J. Harrington.
        p. cm.
    Includes bibliographical references.
    ISBN 1-56548-096-1 (pbk.)
    1. Bible. N.T. Romans—Commentaries. I. Title.
BS2665.3.H36 1997
227'.1077—dc21   97-30289

Printed in Canada

Contents

Introduction

This commentary on Paul's letter to the Romans grew out of a decision to develop a series of Sunday homilies on the lectionary texts from Romans for Year A. About the same time various magazines and newspapers that I read regularly were featuring stories about the new interest in "spirituality" — mainly books and programs ranging from self-help to recreational activities, and presenting a somewhat superficial understanding of spirituality. I define spirituality as how a person stands before God and relates to others and to all creation in light of that basic relationship. And so I set out to reflect on what I regard as the best and most profound statement of Christian spirituality ever written — Paul's letter to the Romans. I was encouraged by the reception given these homilies at St. Peter's Church in Cambridge and at St. Agnes Church in Arlington, Massachusetts. With this book I want to give a more complete and systematic presentation of the topic of Christian spirituality according to Paul's letter to the Romans.

The focus of this exposition of Romans is the "gospel" — the good news of Jesus Christ. It explains what God has done through Jesus Christ, especially in his death and resurrection, and what this means for people of faith. After a general introduction, I provide for each passage in Romans the text according to the *New American Bible* (Revised), an exposition that seeks to clarify Paul's argument with particular attention to its literary and theological dimensions, and suggestions for reflection and discussion (with a final question as a possible starting point). Given the size of Romans (the longest of Paul's letters) and the space limits of the series, I will not repeat features included in my book *Paul's Prison Letters: Philemon, Philippians, and Colossians*, in this series. There I give explanations of literary conventions, cross-references to other Pauline letters, and "spiritual exercises" at the end of each letter.

In this exposition of Romans I want to give special attention to what Paul's spirituality might say to Christians and others at the dawn of the third millennium. My conviction is that we can learn much from Paul about Christian identity, the Church, ecumenism, Christian-Jewish relations, and ecology. I am in basic agreement with Karl Barth's famous statement: "If we rightly understand ourselves, our problems are the problems of Paul; and if we be enlightened by the brightness of his answers, those answers must be ours" (*The Epistle to the Romans*, p. 1).

Paul's Situation

Paul's letters are usually addressed to the Christian communities that he had founded. They were one way of continuing his mission as their founding apostle. But Paul had not founded the church at Rome. The large Jewish community at Rome was the context in which Christianity arose there, and by the early 40s of the first century A.D. it was a lively movement. As non-Jews became part of the Christian movement, some tensions developed between them and Jewish Christians. When Jews (and Jewish Christians) were expelled from Rome in A.D. 49 under the emperor Claudius (see Acts 18:2), Gentile Christians presumably took control of the church there. When Jews were allowed to return to Rome in A.D. 54, the Jewish Christians naturally expected to resume their place of leadership and prominence, and the tensions grew more serious.

Paul wrote his letter to the Romans from Corinth (see 16:21-23) in A.D. 56 or 57. He wanted to spend some time in Rome before beginning a new missionary effort in Spain (see Rom 15:24, 28). Prior to that, he planned to bring to Jerusalem the proceeds of a collection taken up in various Gentile Christian communities in Asia Minor and Greece (see 15:25).

Paul had several purposes in writing to the Romans. He wanted to present to the Roman Christians a synthesis of his gospel that he would proclaim in Spain, perhaps in answer to criticisms and suspicions that had been raised about his teaching. In Jerusalem Paul probably expected not only to present the collection but also to face questioning about his gospel from the local church leaders. In Romans Paul was therefore preparing a systematic defense of the Law-free gospel for non-Jews that he had been preaching. And finally by his exposition of the unity among Gentiles and Jews that Jesus' death and resurrection had created, he very likely intended to help the Roman Christians to deal effectively with their own internal community conflict (see especially 14:1–15:13).

There is no doubt that Paul wrote the letter to the Romans, though he does seem to have employed the services of a scribe named Tertius in doing so (see 16:22). The final warning (16:17-20) and the concluding doxology (16:25-27) may well have been added later to the original list of greetings to Christians at Rome (16:1-16) by those with Paul at Corinth (16:21-23).

Paul's Presupposition

Behind Paul's letter to the Romans there seems to be an intellectual framework that Paul never fully explains. That framework is sometimes called "modified apocalyptic dualism." It is dualism in the sense that there are sharp oppositions (good versus evil, light versus darkness) and little in between. It is modified in that God's sovereignty is presupposed, and the reign of the two opposing powers is temporary and subject to God's plan. It is apocalyptic in that God will bring the dualistic struggle to an end and vindicate the righteous for all creation to see.

The clearest presentation of modified apocalyptic dualism appears in one of the Dead Sea scrolls, *The Rule of the Community*, columns 3–4. That text affirms the sovereignty of God: "From the God of knowledge comes all that is and shall be." It views the present under the two powers: "He [God] has appointed for him [humankind] two spirits in which to walk until the time of his visitation: the spirits of truth and falsehood." The leaders of those who walk by these spirits are the Prince of Light (probably the archangel Michael) and the Angel of Darkness (Satan) respectively. Those who follow the Prince of Light and do the (good) deeds of light are the children of light. Those who follow the Angel of Darkness and do the (evil) deeds of darkness are the children of darkness. In the present the two spirits struggle for dominance over human beings. But "God has ordained an end for falsehood, and at the time of his visitation he will destroy it forever."

This schema of modified apocalyptic dualism can be diagrammed as follows:

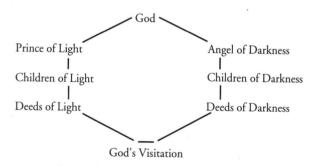

I doubt that Paul himself read *The Rule of the Community*. But he (and John) seems to have thought along the same Jewish apocalyptic lines. Paul too affirms God as creator and Lord of the universe. He too views the time until Christ as a struggle between good and evil. And he too looks forward to God's visitation in which the righteous will be vindicated and the wicked will be condemned. In the light of his Christian faith and his own analysis of the situation, Paul uses some different terms. But the schema is basically the same:

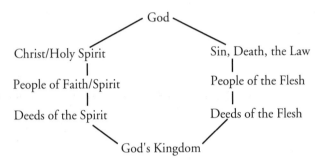

Paul, however, departs from this schema of modified apocalyptic dualism in two dramatic ways. First, by his resurrection from the dead Jesus Christ has anticipated the fullness of God's kingdom and has already triumphed over the hostile forces of sin, death, and the Law. Second, Christ has made it possible for persons of faith who live according to the "spirit" under the direction of the Holy Spirit to enjoy in the present the benefits of God's future kingdom. Through Jesus' death and resurrection they can share in such end-time blessings as justification, peace with God, reconciliation, redemption, and salvation.

Paul's Theological Vocabulary

By Paul's own admission (see 1:3-4, 16-17) the focus of his letter to the Romans is the gospel. With the term "gospel" (*euangelion* in Greek) Paul refers to the good news of Jesus Christ (especially his death and resurrection) and its consequences for human existence. In the body of the letter he deals with the following topics: the definition of the gospel (1:1-17), the universal need for the gospel (1:18–3:20), the gospel and faith (3:21–4:25), the gospel and freedom (5:1–7:25), the gospel and life in the Spirit (8:1-39), the gospel and God's plan (9:1–11:36), the gospel and Christian life (12:1–13:14), the gospel and community conflict (14:1–15:13), and the promotion of the gospel (15:14–16:27).

As Paul develops his reflections on the gospel, he uses certain terms in distinctive ways. What follows are some brief definitions of key Pauline terms. The definitions do not necessarily apply in each and every case. But often enough they do, and so the list may help in understanding Paul's argument. It can serve as a glossary for reference while one works through the exposition that follows.

Body: the whole person, usually in relation to God, others, or the world.

Death: a punishment for sin and personified as a power in league with sin and the Law.

Faith: total trust in God as exemplified by Abraham; the "faith of Christ" may refer to the faith that Christ displayed (subjective genitive) or to faith in Christ (objective genitive).

Flesh: the aspect of the person that is weak and earthly, hostile and in revolt against God. Its opposite is "spirit."

Gentiles: non-Jews; sometimes used for Gentile Christians.

Gospel: the good news of Jesus Christ, especially with reference to his death and resurrection, and its consequences for human beings. Later it becomes the term for the story of Jesus according to Matthew, Mark, Luke, and John.

Justification: the acquittal of humans before the judgment seat of God, brought about even before the last judgment through Jesus' death and resurrection, and thus making righteousness possible.

Law: usually the Mosaic Law, though sometimes a generic term for "principle" or the natural law. Though good and holy in itself, the Mosaic Law becomes an ally of sin and death by revealing to humans what is sin and by inciting them to sin.

Life: the existence conferred on the believer accounted righteous before God and now open to the Holy Spirit's direction.

Righteousness: God's justice made manifest through Christ, anticipating a positive verdict at the last judgment and making possible a new relationship between humans and God (justification).

Salvation: rescue from moral and physical evil in the present and especially in the future kingdom of God.

Related terms include justification, reconciliation, redemption, freedom, sanctification, and glorification.

Sin: sometimes merely a violation of God's will, but more often a power or personification allied with death and the Law.

Spirit: when applied to the human person, "spirit" refers to the person as open to God and striving for life (the opposite of "flesh"). The "Spirit" of God (the Holy Spirit) relates to persons by their "spirit."

World: can be neutral, but often refers to the domain under the power of sin, death, and the Law.

Paul's Problems and Our Problems

In some respects Paul's problems do not seem to be our problems. His presupposition of modified apocalyptic dualism and some issues that concerned him especially (non-Jews as part of God's people, the status of the Mosaic Law, Jewish refusal of the gospel) are far from the consciousness of Christians today. He shows no understanding of the modern concept of homosexuality as a personal orientation (see Rom 1:25-27). He approaches Christian-Jewish relations (see 9–11) without the negative history we bring to this topic today. His political advice (see 13:1-7) may have fit a time when there were about five thousand Christians in the world, but not today when there are about 1.4 billion. And so convinced is he of the absolute significance of Jesus Christ that he leaves little opening for any other way to God.

Despite obvious differences between Paul and us, Paul's letter to the Romans remains a great document of Christian spirituality. If spirituality is defined broadly as how one stands before God and relates to others and to the world in light of this relationship, Romans qualifies as a most extensive and profound presentation of Christian spirituality.

From his own experience of the risen Christ, Paul was convinced that God had acted decisively and definitively through Jesus' death and resurrection, and that this event offered a new way of relating to God. Throughout the letter, Paul explores the significance of Christ "for us" and its many consequences even in the present. He regards Jesus Christ as the key that opens up the Jewish Scriptures. Not only does Jesus Christ fulfill individual texts, but he also stands in the line prepared by great biblical characters such as Adam, Abraham, Moses, David, and Elijah.

Throughout Romans, Paul is concerned with what God is doing in the history of salvation, and with how Jewish Christians, other Jews, and Gentile Christians fit together in God's mysterious plan. Paul cannot imagine the people of God apart from Israel and regards Gentiles as grafted into God's people through Jesus of Nazareth. He encourages Christians to regard their lives as a continuing act of worship, and themselves as members of the body of Christ and of the Spirit-led community.

All of Christian life, according to Paul, flows from what God has done in Christ. All needed the revelation of God's righteousness in Christ, and by faith all can share in its benefits. Through Christ, there is freedom from the power of sin, death, and the Law, and freedom for life in the Spirit. In baptism, Christians enter into the death and life of the crucified and risen Lord. Love is the fulfillment of the Law and enables one to live with respect for the dignity of others.

Despite the obvious differences, I am convinced that Karl Barth's insight is correct at the deepest and most important level. Paul's problems are our problems, and Paul's answers can and should be our answers. To help you to appreciate this dynamic in Romans, let me suggest a simple method of reading and reflecting on Romans. It involves asking and answering four questions: What does the text say? What is God saying to me (or us) through this text? What do I (or we) want to say to God in response? What might God be asking me (or us) to do? What follows should help in answering the first question, and the summary material and question presented for each passage under "For Meditation" may serve as a starting point for dealing with the second question. How one responds to the other two questions is to enter into the challenge of making God's word come alive in our world.

I
The Gospel Defined

The first part of Paul's letter to the Romans follows the conventions of ancient letter-writing. It consists of a greeting (1:1-7), a thanksgiving and a wish (1:8-15), and a statement of the main theme (1:16-17). It is theologically significant because it defines the gospel (1:3-4) and describes the effect of the gospel (1:16-17). Paul presents himself throughout as a minister of the gospel. The unity that Paul finds with the Roman Christians is created by the gospel.

Greeting (1:1-7)

¹Paul, a slave of Christ Jesus, called to be an apostle and set apart for the gospel of God, ²which he promised previously through his prophets in the holy Scriptures, ³the gospel about his Son, descended from David according to the flesh, ⁴but established as Son of God in power according to the spirit of holiness through resurrection from the dead, Jesus Christ our Lord. ⁵Through him we have received the grace of apostleship, to bring about the obedience of faith, for the sake of his name, among all the Gentiles, ⁶among whom are you also, who are called to belong to Jesus Christ; ⁷to all the beloved of God in Rome, called to be holy. Grace to you and

peace from God our Father and the Lord Jesus
Christ.

In Paul's world one began a letter by identifying the
sender ("Paul") and the recipient ("all the beloved of
God in Rome"), and adding a word of greeting ("grace
to you and peace"). The greeting in Romans is note-
worthy for its length and theological substance. Paul
had not founded the church at Rome or even visited
it yet, and some Christians apparently disagreed with
Paul's version of the gospel (see especially Phil, Gal, 2
Cor). And so Paul had to introduce himself in a more
extensive manner and to create common ground with
his readers by appealing to the gospel.

Paul's Christian identity was inextricably connected
to his call from God to preach the gospel: "a slave of
Christ Jesus, called to be an apostle and set apart for
the gospel of God" (1:1). The good news or gospel that
Paul preached had God as its origin and was already
promised in the Jewish Scriptures (1:2). The content
of the gospel is what God has done in Christ Jesus. The
definition of the gospel given in 1:3-4 is generally
viewed as an early Christian summary of faith known
to Paul and the Roman Christians (because of its
parallel structures and unusual vocabulary). It describes Jesus as a descendant of David according to the
flesh (human nature) and as Son of God and Lord
according to the "spirit of holiness" (divine nature). It
identifies Jesus' resurrection from the dead as the
decisive moment in the gospel.

In 1:5-6 Paul explains why he wants to visit the

Roman community and to continue his ministry there and elsewhere. In doing so he links his identity as an apostle with the content of the gospel. The specific grace granted to Paul ("the grace of apostleship") is to bring the gospel of Jesus Christ to non-Jews or Gentiles so that they too might enjoy the "obedience of faith" in accepting the Father of Jesus Christ as their one and only God.

The primary addressees of Paul's letter to the Romans are Gentile Christians (see 1:6). Nevertheless, from the start their dignity as recipients of the gospel is tied to the promises made to Israel through the prophets (1:2). The inclusivity of the gospel is made clear by Paul's combination of the usual Greco-Roman greeting ("grace") and the Jewish greeting ("peace"). Like Paul the Jew, the Roman Christians (a mix of Jews and Gentiles) have been called to belong to Jesus Christ and so deserve to be called "beloved of God" and "holy." They are such not because of their past behavior or their present merits but rather because of the grace and peace bestowed by God through Christ on them.

For Meditation: The unity of Gentiles and Jews in Christ is the chief theme of Paul's letter to the Romans. This unity is shaped by the gospel, and Paul the apostle is its instrument. The unity that Paul envisions is based on God becoming our Father and Jesus becoming our Lord. What good news do Christians today have to offer our world?

Thanksgiving and Wish (1:8-15)

⁸First, I give thanks to my God through Jesus Christ for all of you, because your faith is heralded throughout the world. ⁹God is my witness, whom I serve with my spirit in proclaiming the gospel of his Son, that I remember you constantly, ¹⁰always asking in my prayers that somehow by God's will I may at last find my way clear to come to you. ¹¹For I long to see you, that I may share with you some spiritual gift so that you may be strengthened, ¹²that is, that you and I may be mutually encouraged by one another's faith, yours and mine. ¹³I do not want you to be unaware, brothers, that I often planned to come to you, though I was prevented until now, that I might harvest some fruit among you, too, as among the rest of the Gentiles. ¹⁴To Greeks and non-Greeks alike, to the wise and the ignorant, I am under obligation; ¹⁵that is why I am eager to preach the gospel also to you in Rome.

It was also conventional in Paul's world for letter writers to include after the greeting a thanksgiving and a wish—usually for the good health and prosperity of the recipient. In 1:8 Paul gives thanks to God for the faith of the Roman Christians. As inhabitants of the imperial capital their early adoption of Christianity (probably in the forties of the first century A.D.) must have been well known and thus a stimulus for others to follow their example.

The petition in 1:9-10 uses legal language ("God is my witness," see 9:1) to prepare for the wish that Paul might eventually come to Rome. With expressions that he frequently uses in other letters at this point ("I remember you constantly, always asking in my prayers") Paul seeks to establish a religious bond and a relationship of mutual trust with the Roman Christians, a strategy made necessary by their lack of prior personal contact. The gospel supplies that bond.

The explicit reason for Paul's projected visit to Rome (1:11-12) is to share his spiritual gift ("the grace of apostleship," see 1:5) in confirming the faith of the Roman Christians. Here Paul finds himself in an awkward position. Paul's principle as apostle to the Gentiles was to proclaim the gospel where it had not yet been preached (see 15:20). His other letters provide advice and encouragement to Gentile Christians in communities that he himself had founded. His letter to the Romans is different. He had not founded the community there, and it consists of Gentile and Jewish members. Paul wants to use his visit to Rome as a stop on the way to a projected mission in Spain (see 15:24). Therefore in 1:11-12 Paul's emphasis is on the mutual encouragement in faith that Paul and the Roman Christians can provide one another.

The close relation between Paul's travels and his "grace of apostleship" is further developed in 1:13-15. After a solemn introduction ("I do not want you to be unaware"), he reflects on the tension between his desire to proclaim the gospel everywhere and his failure (as yet) to come to Rome. He portrays his apostolic vocation as a divine necessity and himself under a divine compulsion ("I am under obligation"). The scope of his mission includes all kinds of people: "to Greeks and non-Greeks alike, to the wise and the ignorant" (1:14).

For Meditation: Amidst the literary conventions of the thanksgiving and wish as well as the travel talk, one can feel Paul's love for the gospel and his eagerness to share his "spiritual gift" of being an apostle. The gospel is the chief authority in Paul's life, and he views himself as compelled by God to share the gospel with those who have not heard it and to strengthen the faith of those who have heard it. The bond between Paul and the Roman Christians is the unity created by the gospel. Through his letter and personal presence Paul hopes to strengthen that bond. Is the gospel a source of unity for you?

Main Theme: The Gospel as the Power of God (1:16-17)

> [16] For I am not ashamed of the gospel. It is the power of God for the salvation of everyone who believes: for the Jew first, and then the Greek. [17] For in it is revealed the righteousness of God from faith to faith; as it is written, "The one who is righteous by faith will live."

Paul's major concern in his letter to the Romans is the effect of Jesus' death and resurrection on the lives of those who accept the gospel (soteriology or what Christ means for our salvation). His statement about the "power of the gospel" in 1:16-17 serves as a summary of the entire letter and introduces its main themes.

After an understatement designed to have a positive result ("I am not ashamed of the gospel"), Paul in 1:16

describes the gospel as "the power of God for the salvation of everyone who believes." The gospel whose focus is Jesus' death and resurrection (see 1:3-4) is God's saving gift that is actualized again and again through the Holy Spirit. The goal of the gospel is "salvation." The term refers first of all to a positive verdict at the last judgment that will be part of the fullness of God's kingdom. The benefits of this salvation, however, may be experienced in the present precisely through Christ. Faith understood as trusting God as the origin of the gospel and accepting its content is the way by which Jews and Gentiles alike may participate in the benefits of the gospel.

Since the God of Jesus Christ is the God of Israel, the power of the gospel still respects Israel's preeminence in the history of salvation ("for the Jew first") without excluding others ("and then the Greek"). In fact, Paul's contention throughout Romans is that the gospel is for all peoples. Jesus' death and resurrection has brought about the possibility for all humans to enjoy right relationship with God (justification).

What is revealed in the gospel according to 1:17 is the "righteousness of God." At the root of this expression (as was the case with "salvation" in 1:16) is the idea of the last judgment where God's uprightness or justice will be fully manifest. Paul's point here is that this quality of God has already been displayed in Jesus' death and resurrection. God has taken our side. God is for us. God will be with us.

Again Paul affirms that faith is the sphere in which the gospel works ("from faith to faith"). Here he brings together the themes of righteousness and faith with the quotation of Habakkuk 2:4. In the Hebrew Bible this text ("the righteous shall live by his faith") promised that those who trusted in God would survive a Babylonian attack around 600 B.C. In Romans ("the one who is righteous by faith will live") it refers first to God's positive verdict through Christ on those who believe ("the one who is righteous") and then to the possibility of their enjoying the divine life here and now ("by faith shall live").

For Meditation: The thematic statement in 1:16-17 introduces the key words of the entire letter to the Romans: the gospel as the power of God, salvation, faith, Jews and Greeks, righteousness (divine and human), and life. It also underlines Paul's central concern: the effects of Jesus' death and resurrection on the lives of those who accept and live out the gospel. How do you — individually and communally — experience Jesus Christ as God's good news?

II

The Need for the Gospel

Having defined the gospel in 1:1-17, Paul goes on to explain why all people — Gentiles (1:18-32) and Jews (2:1–3:6) alike — need the gospel. Since Paul was addressing a community made up of Gentile Christians and Jewish Christians, he was inviting all his readers to reflect on their existence before and apart from the gospel. He paints a bleak picture of pagans failing to know God and thus falling into moral degradation (1:18-32), and of Jews relying on their alleged moral superiority (2:1-11), their possession of the Torah (2:12-24), and circumcision (2:25-29). Then, after answering objections to the gospel (3:1-8), he presents an anthology of biblical quotations to illustrate how thoroughly necessary the gospel was (3:9-20). The bleakness of the picture of humankind before and apart from Christ highlights the positive force of the gospel. It is more a theological interpretation than a sociological description.

Gentiles Need the Gospel (1:18-32)

¹⁸ The wrath of God is indeed being revealed from heaven against every impiety and wickedness of those who suppress the truth by their wickedness.

¹⁹For what can be known about God is evident to them, because God made it evident to them. ²⁰Ever since the creation of the world, his invisible attributes of eternal power and divinity have been able to be understood and perceived in what he has made. As a result, they have no excuse; ²¹for although they knew God they did not accord him glory as God or give him thanks. Instead, they became vain in their reasoning, and their senseless minds were darkened.

²²While claiming to be wise, they became fools ²³and exchanged the glory of the immortal God for the likeness of an image of mortal man or of birds or of four-legged animals or of snakes. ²⁴Therefore, God handed them over to impurity through the lusts of their hearts for the mutual degradation of their bodies.

²⁵They exchanged the truth of God for a lie and revered and worshiped the creature rather than the creator, who is blessed forever. Amen. ²⁶Therefore, God handed them over to degrading passions. Their females exchanged natural relations for unnatural, ²⁷and the males likewise gave up natural relations with females and burned with lust for one another. Males did shameful things with males and thus received in their own persons the due penalty for their perversity.

²⁸And since they did not see fit to acknowledge God, God handed them over to their undiscerning mind to do what is improper. ²⁹They are filled with every form of wickedness, evil, greed, and malice; full of envy, murder, rivalry, treachery, and spite. They are gossips and ³⁰scandalmongers and they hate God. They are insolent, haughty, boastful, ingenious in their wickedness, and rebellious toward their parents. ³¹They are senseless, faithless, heartless, ruthless.

[32] Although they know the just decree of God that all who practice such things deserve death, they not only do them but give approval to those who practice them.

Gentiles need the gospel because of their failure to recognize the truth about God and because of the evil behavior that follows from this failure. A mistake about God leads to further ignorance and an evil life (see Wis 13–14). After a statement about God's wrath being revealed in the present (1:18), Paul reflects on the Gentiles' refusal to know God the creator (1:19-21) and on its consequences for their behavior (1:22-32).

Just as salvation can be anticipated in the present (1:16), so according to 1:18 can the wrath of God. The usual context for both terms in Jewish writings of Paul's time is the future judgment that accompanies the fullness of God's kingdom. The "wrath" of God refers to God's indignation against human injustice, cruelty, and corruption. It is the negative aspect of God's justice. Paul sees God's wrath as active also in the present. The proper objects of God's wrath in the present (and the future) are "those who suppress the truth by their wickedness." This truth is the knowledge of God as creator, revealer, and judge. The link between knowledge about God and human behavior is developed in the remainder of the passage.

In 1:19-21 Paul assumes that God can be known from creation — an assumption shared by other religious and philosophical thinkers of his time (see Acts 14:15-17; 17:22-29). What concerns him is that Gentiles have deliberately rejected this "natural theology" and ended in ignorance and moral depravity. After affirming that the invisible and omnipotent God can be recognized from his creatures (1:19-20a), Paul moves quickly to a judgment upon those who rebel against the Lord whom they can and should know: "As a result, they have no excuse" (1:20b). Again in 1:21 Paul emphasizes the reality of the Gentiles' knowledge of God ("they knew God") and their failure to acknowledge and thank this God. The result is even further confusion and ignorance. Here Paul displays not so much a contempt for human reason (one can really know God) as a recognition that human reason becomes clouded by a failure to acknowledge God as creator, revealer, and judge.

In 1:22-32 the idea that failure to acknowledge God led Gentiles into moral perversion is developed in three sequences (1:22-24, 25-27, 28-32). According to 1:22-24 Gentiles who refuse to know God from creation inevitably fall into idolatry, thus mistaking creatures for the creator. This in turn leads to sexual impurity and degradation. Idolatry and moral perversion are the results of rebellion against God.

According to 1:25-27 those who fail to acknowledge the true God and make creatures into their gods inevitably fall into degrading passions. The expression "God handed them over" (1:26; see also 1:24, 28) carries the sense that God let them go their own way so that of their own free will they engage in evil activities. The behavior criticized in this sequence is homosexual activity. What was acceptable in some circles within the Greco-Roman world was rejected by the Jewish Law (see Lv 18:22; 20:13). Paul follows this tradition in condemning promiscuous homosexual conduct (see also 1 Cor 6:9; 1 Tm 1:10). There is no indication that Paul had a concept of homosexual orientation or of a committed and permanent relationship between persons of the same sex.

In the third sequence (1:28-32) a brief mention of the failure to acknowledge God (1:28) is followed in 1:29-31 by a catalogue of vices, a literary form found elsewhere in pagan and Jewish writings. There are four vices listed after "filled with," five vices after "full of," and twelve vices from "gossips" to "ruthless." The point is that a fundamental mistake about God releases a flood of vices that destroys human community and turns creation back to chaos. The final verse (1:32) summarizes the entire passage. In accord with God's just decree those who reject God as their Lord deserve death, which is understood here as a punishment for sin (see Gn 3:19). What Paul finds especially outrageous is that people not only do what appears in the lists of vices but even approve those who do so.

For Meditation: For people today Romans 1:18-32 raises many questions: Was the pagan world as bad as Paul makes it out to be? Is it really so easy to know God from creation? What about moral atheists or agnostics, or observant followers of other religions? Does Paul really understand homosexuality? These important questions should not, however, distract us from Paul's fundamental concern: the relation between knowledge of God and behavior. Paul saw little good in the Gentile world around him. This was in stark contrast to what he believed would happen if Gentiles accepted the gospel and lived according to it. Where do you see signs of the need for the gospel in our world today?

Jews Need the Gospel
Despite Their Moral Superiority (2:1-11)

¹ Therefore, you are without excuse, every one of you who passes judgment. For by the standard by which you judge another you condemn yourself, since you, the judge, do the very same things. ² We know that the judgment of God on those who do such things is true. ³ Do you suppose, then, you who judge those who engage in such things and yet do them yourself, that you will escape the judgment of God?

⁴ Or do you hold his priceless kindness, forebearance, and patience in low esteem, unaware that the kindness of God would lead you to repentance? ⁵ By your stubbornness and impenitent heart, you are storing up wrath for yourself on the day of wrath and revelation of the just judgment of God, ⁶ who will repay everyone according to his works:

⁷ Eternal life to those who seek glory, honor, and immortality through perseverance in good works, ⁸ but wrath and fury to those who selfishly disobey the truth and obey wickedness. ⁹ Yes, affliction and distress will come upon every human being who does evil, Jew first and then Greek. ¹⁰ But there will be glory, honor, and peace for everyone who does good, Jew first and then Greek. ¹¹ There is no partiality with God.

Although Gentile Christians constitute Paul's primary audience in Romans (see 1:4), he often addresses Jewish Christians and non-Christian Jews. Here and in what follows Paul engages in an imaginary debate (technically called a diatribe) with a fellow Jew (see 2:17) who sees no need for the gospel.

The first round in the conversation (2:1-11) concerns the moral superiority that made Judaism attractive to many people in antiquity. In 2:1-3, however, Paul accuses his Jewish debate partner of hypocrisy in passing judgment on others while doing "the very same things" — presumably the vices criticized in 1:18-32. Paul warns that those who have the Jewish Law as a moral guide and recognize and condemn the sins of others in light of it but then commit the same sins will not escape God's judgment (see Mt 7:1; Lk 6:37).

The privilege of being a Jew is to know God's will through the Law and to do it. To presume on God's kindness without repenting from sin (2:4-5; see Wis 15:2, "For even if we sin, we are yours") is to prepare condemnation for oneself at the last judgment. Then God "will repay everyone according to his works" (2:6; see Ps 62:12), and so Jews cannot rely on their privileged status as members of God's people for final salvation.

The relation between one's works and God's verdict at the last judgment is further developed in 2:7-10 with the reward for God's works (2:7, 10) sandwiched around the punishments for evil deeds (2:8-9). In both cases the salvation-historical order ("Jew first and then Greek," see 1:16) is observed. But the real point is that all — Jews and Gentiles alike — will be judged by the same criterion. This idea is confirmed in 2:11 by a quotation of 2 Chronicles 19:7: "There is no partiality with God."

For Meditation: In reading this passage and those that follow one must avoid taking Paul's dialogue partner as a symbol for all Jews or for all religious persons. Rather, Paul is criticizing the ostensibly religious Jew who fails to do what Judaism teaches, presumes on his privileged status as a member of God's people, and condemns those whom he regards as morally inferior. For Paul, such a person was another sign of the need for the gospel. In what does true moral superiority consist?

Jews Need the Gospel Despite Possessing the Torah (2:12-24)

[12] All who sin outside the law will also perish without reference to it, and all who sin under the law will be judged in accordance with it. [13] For it is not those who hear the law who are just in the sight of God; rather, those who observe the law will be justified. [14] For when the Gentiles who do not have the law by nature observe the prescriptions of the law, they are a law for themselves even though they do not have the law. [15] They show that the demands of the law are written in their hearts, while their conscience also bears witness and their conflicting thoughts accuse or even defend them [16] on the day when, according to my gospel, God will judge people's hidden works through Christ Jesus.

17 Now if you call yourself a Jew and rely on the law and boast of God 18 and know his will and are able to discern what is important since you are instructed from the law, 19 and if you are confident that you are a guide for the blind and a light for those in darkness, 20 that you are a trainer of the foolish and teacher of the simple, because in the law you have the formulation of knowledge and truth — 21 then you who teach another, are you failing to teach yourself? You who preach against stealing, do you steal? 22 You who forbid adultery, do you commit adultery? You who detest idols, do you rob temples? 23 You who boast of the law, do you dishonor God by breaking the law? 24 For, as it is written, "Because of you the name of God is reviled among the Gentiles."

The second round in Paul's imaginary conversation with the Jew who sees no need for the gospel (2:12-24) concerns possession of the Jewish Law. The Jewish Law is also known as the Torah, a word that means "instruction" and can refer to the first five books of the Hebrew Bible (the Mosaic Law) or to the entire Old Testament. Here Paul is not criticizing all laws. His meaning is quite specific. Paul's point is that mere possession of the Torah is no guarantee of its observance, nor is it a defense against God's judgment according to one's works.

Whether one sins outside the Law (as a Gentile) or under the Law (as a Jew) is irrelevant. The Jewish ideal, in fact, involves both hearing the Law and acting upon it (see 2:1-11; Jas 1:22-25). Only one who does both will be vindicated at the final judgment (2:13).

In 2:14-16 Paul takes up the case of a Gentile who "naturally" does what the Mosaic Law commands. In view of the bleak picture of the pagan world in 1:18-32, it is possible that here Paul has in mind Gentile Christians. At any rate, Paul envisions the possibility of doing God's will on the basis of the "natural law" written on the human heart (see Jer 31:31-34) and obedience to the dictates of conscience (see Wis 17:11). Such persons too will be vindicated at the last judgment. Note that God's judgment according to one's deeds is part of the gospel (2:16). It is not enough for Jews to presume on possession of the Law; they must do what it teaches. Gentiles cannot plead ignorance of the Law; they have the natural law and conscience as guides, and must follow them.

In 2:17-24 Paul identifies his debating partner explicitly as a "Jew" and lists the privileges of being a Jew. In reading the entire debate or diatribe, one must always keep in mind that Paul the Christian Jew addresses a Jewish debating partner. The five privileges listed in 2:17-18a and the four privileges in 2:19-20a flow from God's gift of the Torah to Israel (see 2:18b, 20b). Because the Jew knows God's will and can instruct others, he is privileged. Thus far Paul and his adversary would be in agreement.

The point of disagreement involves Paul's perception of the Jew's failure to do what the Law requires (see 2:3, 12-13). By five questions in 2:21-23 Paul seeks to expose the nature of that failure. The three sins — stealing, adultery, and temple robbing (probably trafficking in objects taken from pagan temples)

— are sandwiched in 2:21b-22 between the more general accusations in 2:21a and 23. The debate partner is accused of neglecting to teach himself the Law and thus of dishonoring the name of the God of Israel before non-Jews. The accusation is strengthened with a quotation from Isaiah 52:5: "Because of you the name of God is reviled among the Gentiles."

For Meditation: Paul's indictment of his Jewish debate partner for failing to fulfill God's Law was a negative way of trying to make clear the need for God to take a new initiative through Jesus Christ (the gospel). Paul was convinced that the gospel, not the Torah, made possible right relationship with God. Nevertheless, he regarded the gospel as the fulfillment of God's promises to Israel, not the complete rejection of Judaism. Where in your own life (taken individually and/or communally) do you see a failure to act in accord with the wisdom and truth you possess?

Jews Need the Gospel Despite Circumcision (2:25-29)

²⁵ Circumcision, to be sure, has value if you observe the law; but if you break the law, your circumcision has become uncircumcision. ²⁶ Again, if an uncircumcised man keeps the precepts of the law, will he not be considered circumcised? ²⁷ Indeed, those who are physically uncircumcised but carry out the law will pass judgment on you, with your written law and circumcision, who break the law. ²⁸ One is not a Jew outwardly. True circumcision is not outward, in the flesh. ²⁹ Rather, one is a Jew inwardly, and circumcision is of the heart, in the

spirit, not the letter; his praise is not from human beings but from God.

The next round in the conversation (2:25-29) concerns circumcision — a practice known in other cultures but in Paul's time regarded as distinctively Jewish. So much was circumcision viewed as a special sign of being a Jew and thus making one part of God's people that the word "covenant" was sometimes used as a synonym for it.

In 2:25 Paul rejects the assumption that circumcision has saving power. Rather, it has power only for those who faithfully observe the precepts of the covenant. Then in 2:26-27 Paul goes back to the case of the non-Jew who by "nature" does what the Torah commands (see 2:14-15). Such a person deserves to be a member of God's covenant people and thus considered "circumcised" (2:26). Such a one, in fact, is morally superior to the Jew who is physically circumcised and possesses the written Law but fails to act upon it (2:27). Here Paul is clearly moving toward a spiritual understanding of circumcision as openness to God.

In 2:28-29 Paul does spiritualize both "circumcision" and "Jew": The true member of God's covenant people (the true Jew) is one inwardly rather than externally (by physical circumcision), and the true circumcision concerns the heart rather than the male member. The spiritual character of these realities is emphasized by the oppositions between spirit and letter, and between praise from God and praise from human beings.

For Meditation: Paul criticizes his debate partner for presuming on his status as a member of God's covenant people (symbolized by circumcision) and for failing to do what that status requires. (Some Christians seem to attribute the same power to baptism and neglect doing what Christian faith requires.) This in turn leads Paul to define membership in God's people to include all who do God's will (including non-Jews). Thus Paul leaves open membership in God's people to Gentile Christians (Paul's chief concern in Romans) and perhaps to all people of good will and good action (the modern Christian concern with the "anonymous Christian"). How do you define the people of God, and what are the most important criteria for membership?

Objections and Answers (3:1-8)

¹ What advantage is there then in being a Jew? Or what is the value of circumcision? ² Much, in every respect. For in the first place, they were entrusted with the utterances of God.

³ What if some were unfaithful? Will their infidelity nullify the fidelity of God? ⁴ Of course not! God must be true, though every human being is a liar, as it is written: "That you may be justified in your words, and conquer when you are judged."

⁵ But if our wickedness provides proof of God's righteousness, what can we say? Is God unjust, humanly speaking, to inflict his wrath? ⁶ Of course not! For how else is God to judge the world? ⁷ But if God's truth redounds to his glory through my falsehood, why am I still being condemned as a sinner? ⁸ And why not say — as we are accused and as some

claim we say — that we should do evil that good may come of it? Their penalty is what they deserve.

Thus far in the debate Paul has taken the offensive against his Jewish partner. Paul has exposed the folly of relying on the claim of moral superiority, mere possession of the Torah, and circumcision as the sign of belonging to God's people. In 3:1-8 the format and tone change, and Paul presents possible objections to his teaching and responds to them. The objections concern the privileged status of Israel (3:1-2), the faithfulness of God (3:3-4), and the justice of God (3:5-8).

The first objection (3:1-2) concerns the value of being a Jew and of circumcision. Throughout chapter 2, Paul showed that these do not guarantee salvation before God. In what, then, does Israel's privilege consist? It consists in Israel being entrusted with "the utterances of God" (3:2). With the gift of the Scriptures God has deposited with Israel the promises that find their fulfillment in the gospel — in the life, death, and resurrection of Jesus Christ. Israel's primary privilege resides in its role in salvation history in preparing for the gospel.

The second objection (3:3-4) concerns the fidelity of God. The question is whether the faithlessness of Israel exposed in chapter 2 nullifies God's faithfulness. Paul's answer is a resounding "Of course not!" He confirms his response first by alluding to Psalm 116:11: "God must be true, though every human being is a liar." Then he quotes Psalm 51:6 in which "you" must refer to God. In every trial (taken in the legal sense, with an eye toward the last judgment) God emerges as just and victorious. The question of God's fidelity is treated at length in chapters 9–11.

The third objection (3:5-8) deals with justice of God. That topic was already raised in 3:4 with the quotation from Psalm 51:6. The objection here arises from Paul's insistence in 1:18–2:29 that the sins of Gentiles and Jews alike show the need for the gospel. The first form of the objection (3:5-6) contends that if human sinfulness highlights the uprightness of God, then it would be unjust for God to hold sinners accountable at the judgment. Paul sweeps away the objection by asserting that God as judge of the world has the duty to judge each person justly, and that therefore God must be just.

The second form of the third objection (3:7-8) restates the idea of the injustice of God in condemning sinners if sin shows the need for the gospel. It goes on to insinuate that according to Paul's teaching one might conclude that "we should do evil that good may come of it" (3:8). The logic is this: Since the revelation of God's righteousness in Christ (see 1:16-17) was a response to humankind's sinfulness and inability to achieve justice before God, it follows that doing evil (sinning) has a good result (the gospel). So absurd does Paul regard this objection that he refuses even to dignify it with a direct answer. Instead, he breaks off the conversation with what is almost a curse or oath against those who indulge such foolish thoughts: "Their penalty is what they deserve." In other words, those who question God's justice and twist Paul's teaching on it will experience God's justice at the last judgment.

For Meditation: Here Paul insists on the privileged status of Israel, the fidelity of God despite human infidelity, and the justice of God. All three he sees fulfilled in, not abrogated by, the gospel of Jesus Christ. These themes will be the subject of large sections in the rest of Romans. How have you experienced God's faithfulness despite your unfaithfulness?

The Universal Domination of Sin (3:9-20)

[9] Well, then, are we better off? Not entirely, for we have already brought the charge against Jews and Greeks alike that they are all under the domination of sin, [10] as it is written: "There is no one just, not one; [11] there is no one who understands, there is no one who seeks God. [12] All have gone astray; all alike are worthless; there is not one who does good, there is not even one. [13] Their throats are open graves; they deceive with their tongues; the venom of asps is on their lips; [14] their mouths are full of bitter cursing. [15] Their feet are quick to shed blood; [16] ruin and misery are in their ways, [17] and the way of peace they know not. [18] There is no fear of God before their eyes."

[19] Now we know that what the law says is addressed to those under the law, so that every mouth may be silenced and the whole world stand accountable to God, [20] since no human being will be justified in his sight by observing the law; for through the law comes consciousness of sin.

In 3:9 Paul returns to the issue of the qualitative advantage of being a Jew (see 3:1). He has argued that before God Jews are not entirely better off than Gentiles. The reason is that, before and apart from Christ, Jews and Gentiles alike were "under the domination of sin." Here (and especially in chapters 5–7) sin is almost personified. Paul cannot imagine a human being without a lord or master. His point here is that without Christ both Jews and Gentiles found themselves under sin's lordship.

How completely humans were under sin's domination is made clear by an anthology of biblical quotations in 3:10-18. The first two quotations establish that "no one is just" (3:10b = Eccl 7:20) and that there is no one "who understands . . . who seeks God . . . who does good" (3:11-12 = Ps 14:1-3; 53:2-4). The remaining quotations (3:13-18) focus on various parts of the body and their corruption by sin: throats (3:13a-b = Ps 5:10), lips (3:13c = Ps 140:4), mouths (3:14 = Ps 10:7), feet (3:15-17 = Is 59:7-8; Prv 1:16), and eyes (3:18 = Ps 36:2). This combination of the biblical texts is intended to show that, before and apart from Christ, each and every person was under the domination of sin.

As a conclusion to his anthology of biblical texts, Paul in 3:19 makes explicit that the Law itself — understood here as including all the Jewish Scriptures — supports his theological analysis about the universal lordship of sin. Then in 3:20 he moves forward the argument by raising two issues that he will soon treat in more detail: the Law's inability to bring about right relationship with God (justification), and the Law's role in bringing about knowledge of sin (see 5:13, 20). At many points, Paul perceives the Law as part of the alliance between sin and death.

For Meditation: From the Jewish Scriptures Paul establishes that Jews and Gentiles alike needed someone or something beyond their own human wisdom and efforts, and even beyond the Torah revealed to Israel, to bring about right relationship with God. According to Paul, only Jesus Christ, the Son of God, who died for us, could achieve what was necessary. Throughout 1:18–3:20 Paul's bleak picture of human existence before and apart from Christ highlights the necessity for the revelation of God's righteousness in the event celebrated by the gospel. Is Paul an optimist or a pessimist?

III

The Gospel and Faith

Having demonstrated that both Gentiles and Jews needed the gospel of Jesus Christ as the revelation of God's righteousness, Paul first establishes the relation between the gospel and faith (3:21-26) and explains why no human can take credit for what God has done through Christ (3:27-31). Then he reflects on Abraham as a model of what faith and justification mean. He shows that Abraham was justified by faith (4:1-8) before and apart from circumcision (4:9-12) and the Mosaic Law (4:13-17), and so is an example for us all — Jews and Gentiles — as we accept the gospel and live by it (4:18-25).

God's Righteousness and Faith (3:21-26)

[21] But now the righteousness of God has been manifested apart from the law, though testified to by the law and the prophets, [22] the righteousness of God through faith in Jesus Christ for all who believe. For there is no distinction; [23] all have sinned and are deprived of the glory of God. [24] They are justified freely by his grace through the redemption in Christ Jesus, [25] whom God set forth as an expiation, through faith, by his blood, to prove his righteousness because of the

44

forgiveness of sins previously committed, [26]through the forebearance of God — to prove his righteousness in the present time, that he might be righteous and justify the one who has faith in Jesus.

Having established the desperate condition of humankind before and apart from Christ, Paul in 3:21-22a moves on to explain what God has done in and through Jesus' death and resurrection. As already stated in 1:16-17, Paul interprets the Christ-event or gospel as the revelation of God's righteousness. Whereas in Jewish writings of Paul's time the revelation of God's righteousness was expected on the future Day of the Lord, Paul (and other early Christians) believed this to have been anticipated in Jesus Christ, and that therefore some of the benefits of God's kingdom in its fullness (especially freedom from the domination of sin) can be experienced and enjoyed in the present.

Two other important themes appear in 3:21-22a. The Mosaic Law is definitely not on the same level as the gospel as God's way of justification, and so God's righteousness has been made manifest in Christ "apart from the law." Although the Law cannot do what Christ has done, the Law and the Prophets do serve as privileged witnesses to what God has done in Christ. And so throughout Romans, Paul is concerned with Christ as the fulfillment of the Jewish Scriptures.

The second subsidiary theme in 3:21-22a is faith as the way by which humans become part of the Christ-event: "the righteousness of God through faith in Jesus Christ for all who believe" (3:22a; see 1:17). According to the *New American Bible* (Revised) and most other translations, "Jesus Christ" is taken as an objective genitive; that is, "faith in Jesus Christ," Christ as the object of faith. But it is also possible (and preferable, I think) to take it as a subjective genitive; that is, "the faith of Jesus Christ," the faith that he possessed and showed toward his heavenly Father, and the good example of faithfulness that he gave to us.

In 3:22b-23 Paul repeats (see 1:18–3:20) the reason why God's righteousness was made manifest in Christ. All humans stood under the domination of sin and so had no claim on or right to the glory of God's kingdom. The expression "all have sinned" (see 5:12) describes more than personal sin. Rather, it refers to the power of sin (almost personified) over all human beings ("there is no distinction").

What Jesus' death and resurrection mean for us is explained with various images in 3:24. The first image is legal ("they are justified"). The background is the idea of the last judgment, and the claim is that even before the last judgment — in the here and now through Christ — God has declared those who believe to be righteous or just. The second image ("freely by his grace") emphasizes the generosity of God in making this possible and rejects any claim that we deserve justification through our own merits. The third image ("redemption") carries the idea of the change of lords from sin to God that has taken place through Christ. God has graciously taken the initiative in our justification and redemption by making manifest his own righteousness in Christ.

46

The language and content (apart from "through faith") of 3:25-26a ("whom God set forth . . . the forbearance of God") suggest that an early Christian credal formula is quoted to establish common theological ground between Paul and the Roman Christians (as in 1:3-4). The formula interprets Christ's death as an expiatory sacrifice (see Lv 16:13-16). The need for such a sacrifice arose from humankind's hostility to God and its dominion by sin (see 3:22b-23). The sacrificial death of Christ ("by his blood") appears as the offering provided by God ("whom God set forth") as a means of wiping away sin (as at the Day of Atonement) and giving a new beginning to humankind. The idea of Christ's death as an expiatory sacrifice is rooted in the figure of the Suffering Servant (see Is 52:13–53:12) and is fully developed from a Christian theological perspective in the letter to the Hebrews.

To this credal formula, Paul in 3:25 ("through faith") and 3:26b ("to prove . . . faith in Jesus") adds his interpretive comments: (1) Faith is the way by which humans participate in the drama of the gospel ("through faith . . . one who has faith"). Whether this faith has Jesus as its object or subject (see 3:22) is again ambiguous. (2) Through Christ's death and resurrection, God's righteousness is manifest "in the present time," not reserved for the future Day of the Lord. (3) The righteousness of God is the basis for God's declaring and making righteous (justifying) sinful humankind: "that he might be righteous and justify." This justification is grounded in Christ's death as the manifestation of God's righteousness.

For Meditation: Paul's main concern in Romans is the effect of Jesus' death and resurrection on us. In other words, he approaches Christology with a focus on soteriology (what Christ means for our salvation). In 3:21-26 — one of the richest and most important passages in the entire letter — Paul opens up many aspects of the significance of the Christ-event for us: the revelation of God's righteousness, fulfillment of the Scriptures, justification, grace, redemption, expiation, sacrifice, and forgiveness of sins. He also stresses faith as the way by which we participate in what the gospel proclaims. Which of these images helps you most to appreciate what God has done for us in Christ?

No Grounds for Boasting (3:27-31)

²⁷ What occasion is there then for boasting? It is ruled out. On what principle, that of works? No, rather on the principle of faith. ²⁸ For we consider that a person is justified by faith apart from works of the law.

²⁹ Does God belong to Jews alone? Does he not belong to Gentiles, too? Yes, also to Gentiles, ³⁰ for God is one and will justify the circumcised on the basis of faith and the uncircumcised through faith.

³¹ Are we then annulling the law by this faith? Of course not! On the contrary, we are supporting the law.

In the course of restating the main points made in the previous passage, Paul reverts to the question and answer format (3:27-28, 29-30, 31) as in 2:1-29. Also, instead of using the word for "law" (*nomos*) only in its usual sense in Romans as the Mosaic Law, here he gives it three different meanings: principle (3:27), the Mosaic Law (3:28), and God's deepest intention or will (3:31).

The first round of questions and answers (3:27-28) denies that any human can boast of right relationship with God (justification). The reason is that justification is a matter of faith rather than human achievements (works). It is based on the principle (*nomos*) of faith: "a person is justified by faith apart from the works of the law" (3:28; see 3:21-26) — with "law" here referring to the Mosaic Law. Because justification is God's gift, no human can take credit for it. For Paul, faith is not a human work but the proper response to God's initiative that in turn issues in good works.

The second round (3:29-30) makes the same point in the context of salvation history. There is only one God (see Dt 6:4), and this God must encompass both Jews and Gentiles. And for Jews and Gentiles alike there is only one way of relating to God — through faith (as the example of Abraham in chapter 4 will show).

In the third round (3:31) Paul raises an issue that he will treat again: "Are we then annulling the law by this faith?" In answering the question Paul once more shifts the meaning of "law" (*nomos*). Here it refers to what God really intended through the Mosaic Law. Paul views the positive contribution of the Law as a witness in preparation for the gospel (see 3:21). And so he can assert that in proclaiming the gospel, he does not annul the Law but rather supports it in its deepest sense as God's will made manifest.

For Meditation: Justification (right relationship with God) is primarily God's gift, and we enjoy that gift by faith. Therefore taking credit for, or boasting about, our religious achievements is both foolish and insulting to God. Of course, faith demands good actions by way of response. But the real credit belongs to God, through Christ. Do you ever consider what God has done for you, and praise and thank God in return?

Abraham Justified by Faith (4:1-8)

[1] What then can we say that Abraham found, our ancestor according to the flesh? [2] Indeed, if Abraham was justified on the basis of his works, he has reason to boast; but this was not so in the sight of God. [3] For what does Scripture say? "Abraham believed God, and it was credited to him as righteousness."

[4] A worker's wage is credited not as a gift, but as something due. [5] But when one does not work, yet believes in the one who justifies the ungodly, his faith is credited as righteousness.

[6] So also David declares the blessedness of the person to whom God credits righteousness apart from works: [7] "Blessed are they whose iniquities are forgiven and whose sins are covered. [8] Blessed is the man whose sin the Lord does not record."

To prove his thesis that justification is by faith rather than by the works of the Law (that is, merely doing what the Law says), Paul focuses on Abraham and calls upon various biblical texts. By describing

Abraham as "our ancestor according to the flesh" (4:1), Paul underlines the physical ties between the patriarch and Jews of Paul's own day. And yet there is some irony here, since the goal of Paul's argument is to show that Abraham is father of all believers and not merely of Jews (see 4:16). He admits in 4:2 that, even if Abraham had been justified by his works, he might have reason to boast before humans — but surely not before God (see 3:27-28). In fact, Abraham is the perfect example of Paul's thesis of justification by faith.

In 4:3 Paul takes as his biblical starting point Genesis 15:6: "Abraham believed God, and it was credited to him as righteousness." The original context is God's promise to Abraham that he would have a son (Isaac) and through him many offspring. Because Abraham trusted in God's promise, he was regarded as righteous before God. The verb "credited" carries a business connotation, evoking the sense of a decision made by the chief "bookkeeper." But the principle on which the books are kept is faith, not the works of the Law. According to Paul, Abraham's righteousness consisted in accepting God's word and living according to it without reservation. His faith was a radical trust in God.

In 4:4 Paul explains his thesis further with the help of another business analogy. When someone does a job and gets paid for it, the pay is a wage rather than a gift. By way of contrast in 4:5 he applies the analogy to Abraham as he is described in Genesis 15:6. Abraham's being declared righteous by God was based on his faith in God's promise, not on his works. Therefore it was a gift rather than something owed to him. God dealt with Abraham in the realm of faith rather than of works. The "ungodly" whom God justifies encompasses all humankind under the domination of sin (which therefore has no claim on God and no right to boast before God).

That God deals in the realm of grace and faith rather than in that of works is confirmed in 4:6-8 by the testimony of David, the traditional author of the Psalms, and (with Abraham and Moses) one of the most respected figures in the biblical tradition. The quotation from Psalm 32:1-2 in 4:7-8 develops the theme of God as "the one who justifies the ungodly" (see 4:5). It declares "happy" or "blessed" those whose sins God has forgiven. Here Paul is probably more interested in the freedom from the power of sin that has occurred through Jesus' death and resurrection than in the forgiveness of personal sins.

For Meditation: The essence of Abraham's faith, according to Paul, is trust in God, acceptance of God's promise, and life in accord with God's word. How do you define faith?

Abraham Justified Before Circumcision (4:9-12)

⁹Does this blessedness apply only to the circumcised, or to the uncircumcised as well? Now we assert that "faith was credited to Abraham as righteousness." ¹⁰Under what circumstances was it credited? Was he circumcised or not? He was not circumcised, but uncircumcised.

¹¹And he received the sign of circumcision as a seal on the righteousness received through faith while he was uncircumcised. Thus he was to be the father of all the uncircumcised who believe, so that to them also righteousness might be credited, ¹²as well as the father of the circumcised who not only are circumcised but also follow the path of faith that our father Abraham walked while still uncircumcised.

In 4:9 Paul takes up the possible objection that David's blessing on those whose sins God has forgiven (Ps 32:1-2 = Rom 4:7-8) applied only to Jews. He first appeals to the statement in Genesis 15:6 that Abraham's faith was the basis for his justification. Then in 4:10 he asks whether Abraham was declared righteous before or after he was circumcised. According to the chronology of Genesis, Abraham was circumcised twenty-nine years after the declaration made in Genesis 15:6 (see Gn 17:10-27). Therefore Abraham's justification took place before circumcision was introduced and so had nothing to do with it.

What then was the function of circumcision in God's plan? In 4:11a Paul describes it as a "sign" and a "seal" of the righteousness that Abraham had received earlier without having been circumcised. According to Paul, Abraham's circumcision was the confirmation and documentation of his right relationship with God. From this Paul concludes in 4:11b-12 that Abraham deserves to be regarded as the father of all those who believe as he did. Righteousness and faith after the pattern of Abraham are possible for both

Gentiles and Jews (note the reversal of the usual salvation historical order). In 4:12 Paul returns to the theme that circumcision by itself does not result in justification (see 2:25-29). The circumcised (Jews) must also follow the way of faith that Abraham walked (Gn 15:6) even before his circumcision (Gn 17:10-27).

For Meditation: Paul reads the Abraham stories in Genesis through the lens of the gospel and gives a Christian interpretation of them. Nevertheless, the three great monotheistic religions — Judaism, Christianity, and Islam — all take Abraham as their father in faith. How can the figure of Abraham bring together Jews, Christians, and Muslims today?

Abraham Justified Before the Law (4:13-17)

[13] It was not through the law that the promise was made to Abraham and his descendants that he would inherit the world, but through the righteousness that comes from faith. [14] For if those who adhere to the law are the heirs, faith is null and the promise is void. [15] For the law produces wrath; but where there is no law, neither is there violation. [16] For this reason, it depends on faith, so that it may be a gift and the promise may be guaranteed to all his descendants, not to those who only adhere to the law but to those who follow the faith of Abraham, who is the father of all of us, [17] as it is written, "I have made you a father of many nations." He is our father in the sight of God, in whom he believed, who gives life to the dead and calls into being what does not exist.

54

Abraham was declared righteous not only before circumcision but also before the giving of the Law to Moses on Mount Sinai (see Ex 19 ff.). Therefore, Abraham's justification was also before and apart from the Law. Moreover, the promise made to Abraham that he and his offspring would inherit the land of Israel (see Gn 22:17-18) and even the world (see Sir 44:21) was prior to and apart from the Law.

The "righteousness that comes from faith" was the sphere in which Abraham's acceptance of God's promise became possible (4:13), whereas those who remain under the Law as the way to right relationship with God nullify both the faith and the promise (4:14). Here Paul begins to develop his negative characterization of the Mosaic Law as a personified power allied with sin and death. In 4:15 he also raises the idea of the Law as bringing knowledge of sin and enticement to sin. The Law produces the violations that in turn merit God's wrath at the judgment.

According to 4:16-17, the promise made to Abraham and the faith that he displayed concern not only Jews (those physical descendants who adhere to the Law) but also Gentiles (those spiritual descendants who follow Abraham's example of faith). The reason is that Abraham is "the father of all of us" — a title based on the promise that God would make him "the father of many nations" (Gn 17:5).

Abraham's spiritual fatherhood, according to Paul, is not a vague universalism. Rather, it embraces all who believe the gospel. For Paul (4:17b), the proper object of faith is the God who gives life to the dead (the one who raised Jesus from the dead as the pledge of our resurrection) and who continually brings about the new creation (inaugurated by Jesus' death and resurrection).

For Meditation: The proper object of faith after the pattern of Abraham is the gospel of Jesus Christ. Here Paul stresses the opposition between God's promise and faith on the one hand and the Mosaic Law on the other hand. Again, the aim is to highlight the positive significance of the gospel. Is it correct to call Abraham the first Christian?

Abraham as Example of Faith (4:18-25)

18 He believed, hoping against hope, that he would become "the father of many nations," according to what was said, "Thus shall your descendants be." 19 He did not weaken in faith when he considered his own body as already dead (for he was almost a hundred years old) and the dead womb of Sarah. 20 He did not doubt God's promise in unbelief; rather, he was empowered by faith and gave glory to God 21 and was fully convinced that what he had promised he was also able to do. 22 That is why "it was credited to him as righteousness."

23 But it was not for him alone that it was written that "it was credited to him"; 24 it was also for us, to whom it will be credited, who believe in the one who raised Jesus our Lord from the dead, 25 who was handed over for our transgressions and was raised for our justification.

In 4:18-22 Paul explores the nature of Abraham's faith. God's promise that Abraham would become the father of many nations through a son (Isaac) and that his descendants would be as numerous as the stars in the sky (see Gn 15:15) seemed impossible. The reason was the advanced ages of Abraham — one hundred years — and Sarah — ninety years — according to Genesis 17:17. Despite what seemed totally unrealistic, Abraham "hoped against hope" (4:18) and "did not weaken in faith" (4:19). He was "empowered by faith and gave glory to God" (4:20), so "fully convinced" (4:21) was he that God could and would fulfill the promise. From Paul's perspective, Abraham's call to be the father of many nations foreshadowed the spreading of the gospel of Jesus Christ to the Gentiles. For their part, non-Jews could become part of God's people by imitating Abraham's example of faith in God's promise (the gospel). Just as Abraham's faith was the basis for his justification (see Gn 15:6), so the Gentiles' acceptance of the gospel would mean right relationship with God for them (4:22).

In 4:23-25 Paul moves from interpreting biblical texts to making explicit Abraham's case according to Gn 15:6 for us: "But it was not for him alone . . . it was also for us." The "righteousness that comes from faith" (4:13) links Abraham to all those — Jews and Gentiles alike — who accept the gospel of Jesus Christ. The God whose promise Abraham trusted is the one who raised Jesus from the dead. Our response should be that of Abraham (faith) so that the result might also be the same (justification).

The long reflection on the gospel and faith (3:21–4:25) closes in 4:25 with what seems to have been another early Christian credal summary (see 1:3-4; 3:25-26a). It proclaims the gospel in terms of Jesus' sacrificial death ("handed over for our transgressions," see Is 53:5, 12) and resurrection ("raised for our justification"). Note that this summary of the gospel includes theological interpretations of Jesus' death (forgiveness of sins) and resurrection (justification).

For Meditation: Paul connects Abraham's faith and his justification directly to the gospel of Jesus Christ. In describing Abraham's faith, he emphasizes the gap between what Abraham was asked to accept as God's promise and what seemed realistic. And yet Abraham accepted God's promise and was vindicated by the birth of Isaac and eventually by the revelation of God's righteousness in Jesus Christ. Have you ever displayed something like Abraham's faith in your own life?

IV

The Gospel and Freedom

One of the earliest expressions of Christian faith proclaimed that "Christ died for our sins" (1 Cor 15:3; see Rom 3:25; 4:25). Paul greatly deepened this theological interpretation of Jesus' death. He took the word "sin" to refer not simply to personal sins but rather to the power that held humankind in its deathly grip. In Romans 5–7 he reflects on how God through Christ's death and resurrection freed humankind from the dominion of sin, death, and the Law. His main biblical source is Genesis 2–3, and he makes much out of the similarities and differences between Adam and Christ. Though the three powers cannot be separated, Paul focuses on sin in chapter 5, death in chapter 6, and the Law in chapter 7.

What God Has Done in Christ (5:1-11)

[1] Therefore, since we have been justified by faith, we have peace with God through our Lord Jesus Christ, [2] through whom we have gained access by faith to this grace in which we stand, and we boast in the hope of the glory of God.

[3] Not only that, but we even boast of our afflictions, knowing that affliction produces endurance,

⁴and endurance, proven character, and proven character, hope, ⁵and hope does not disappoint, because the love of God has been poured out into our hearts through the Holy Spirit that has been given to us.

⁶For Christ, while we were still helpless, yet died at the appointed time for the ungodly. ⁷Indeed, only with difficulty does one die for a just person, though perhaps for a good person one might even find courage to die. ⁸But God proves his love for us in that while we were still sinners Christ died for us.

⁹How much more then, since we are now justified by his blood, will we be saved through him from the wrath. ¹⁰Indeed, if, while we were enemies, we were reconciled to God through the death of his Son, how much more, once reconciled, will we be saved by his life. ¹¹Not only that, but we also boast of God through our Lord Jesus Christ, through whom we have now received reconciliation.

Paul shared with his Jewish contemporaries the idea of the future kingdom of God and the future judgment according to one's deeds (see 2:6). But Paul (and other early Christians) was convinced that the sharp division between the present ("this age") and the future ("the age to come") had broken down through Jesus' death and resurrection. And so it is possible through Christ for believers to enjoy the benefits of God's kingdom in the present, without losing hope for their fullness in the future.

In 5:1-2 Paul begins to mention some of those benefits. Justification ("justified by faith") means that those who accept Christ as their Lord and as the revelation of God's righteousness have already received a positive judgment from God (acquittal) and so can now stand in right relationship with God. No longer under the power of sin and now in Christ, such persons enjoy "peace with God" — not the uneasy cessation of hostility that characterizes most human peace treaties but rather peace as the foretaste of the fullness of salvation. Through Christ we also have "access" to God. The image evokes the idea of gaining admission to a king's court or to the holiest part of a temple. Though we cannot take credit for our own salvation (see 3:27-31), we can "boast in hope of the glory of God" (the fullness of God's kingdom) while enjoying the favor of God in the present ("this grace in which we stand").

Rather than ignoring suffering or explaining it away as illusory, Paul in 5:3-5 looks on suffering as part of the present reality. Building around what was probably a traditional piece that links affliction, endurance, proven character, and hope (5:3b-5a), Paul views suffering as something about which one can boast (because Christ suffered too) and as of secondary importance when compared to what God has done in Christ. Through the event celebrated in the gospel, the "love of God" (God's love for us) has taken hold of our inmost self through the gift of the Holy Spirit, which in turn makes suffering bearable.

In 5:6-8 Paul defines God's love for us in terms of Christ's death on the cross. The terms "helpless" and "ungodly" in 5:6 and "sinners" in 5:8 describe humankind under the power of sin — a theme developed at length in 1:18–3:20. In 5:7 Paul invokes an analogy to highlight the greatness of God's love for us in Christ.

We celebrate as heroic someone who is willing to sacrifice his or her life for another (usually a good and righteous person, a friend, or a child). How much more should we celebrate Christ's death on behalf of "sinners"! His death took place according to God's plan ("at the appointed time") and is proof of God's love for us (see 8:32). By dying for us, Christ made it possible for us to move out from under the power of sin and to enjoy the present benefits of God's kingdom (see 5:1-2).

In 5:9-11 Paul returns to the theme of the benefits of the Christ-event in terms of the present and future kingdom of God. Since Christ's death ("by his blood") is the instrument of our justification, we can be confident of a positive final judgment and so need not fear "the wrath" (5:9). Here justification and salvation describe the present and future destiny of the Christian. In 5:10-11 Paul uses the terms reconciliation and salvation to make the same point. It is legitimate to boast of these actions of God in Christ.

For Meditation: Throughout Romans, Paul's fundamental concern is what God has done for us in Christ. In 5:1-11 he mentions some of the present benefits of the event celebrated in the gospel: justification by faith, peace with God, access to God, standing in God's favor (grace), God's love in our hearts, freedom from the power of sin, and reconciliation with God. And yet Paul retains the vision of the future fullness of God's kingdom, and so he speaks of the "hope of the glory of God" (5:2) and being saved "from the wrath . . . by his life" (5:9-10). Which of the many benefits of the Christ-event is most important in your spiritual life?

Adam and Christ (5:12-21)

[12]Therefore, just as through one person sin entered the world, and through sin, death, and thus death came to all, inasmuch as all sinned — [13]for up to the time of the law, sin was in the world, though sin is not accounted when there is no law. [14]But death reigned from Adam to Moses, even over those who did not sin after the pattern of the trespass of Adam, who is the type of the one who was to come.

[15]But the gift is not like the transgression. For if by that one person's transgression the many died, how much more did the grace of God and the gracious gift of the one person Jesus Christ overflow for the many. [16]And the gift is not like the result of the one person's sinning. For after one sin there was the judgment that brought condemnation; but the gift, after many transgressions, brought acquittal.

[17]For if, by the transgression of one person, death came to reign through that one, how much more will those who receive the abundance of grace and of the gift of justification come to reign in life through the one person Jesus Christ.

[18]In conclusion, just as through one transgression condemnation came upon all, so through one righteous act acquittal and life came to all. [19]For just as through the disobedience of one person the many were made sinners, so through the obedience of one the many will be made righteous.

[20]The law entered in so that transgression might increase but, where sin increased, grace overflowed all the more, [21]so that, as sin reigned in death, grace

might also reign through justification for eternal life through Jesus Christ our Lord.

In 5:12-21 — one of the most famous passages in the New Testament mainly because of its teaching on "original sin" — Paul develops the similarities and differences between Adam and Christ. They are alike in that both are bearers of a fate or destiny that affects all humans. They differ in that the effect of Adam's sin in disobeying God's command is sin and death, whereas the effect of Christ's sacrificial fidelity to his heavenly Father is grace and life. The central affirmation appears in 5:15a: "But the gift is not like the transgression."

In 5:12 Paul focuses on Adam's sin as it is described in Genesis 3. He takes it as not just a personal sin but as the transgression of a divine command that has influenced all humans. Through Adam's sin, the "powers" of sin and death broke into our world and took control over it. Here death appears as the consequence and ally of sin (see Gn 3:19). All humans repeat the experience of Adam ("inasmuch as all sinned"), and so share Adam's guilt. A Jewish apocalypse somewhat later than Paul's letter to the Romans makes the same point: "Each of us has become our own Adam" (2 *Baruch* 54:19).

According to 5:13-14, even before the Law was given to Moses (which made possible precise knowledge of sin and so also the accounting or tallying of sins, see 4:15), sin and death had power over humankind. Although those who lived between Adam and Moses may not have had a specific precept to violate as Adam did (see Gn 2:17) or as the Law of Moses provided in abundance, they too were under the power of sin and death, and so continued to repeat Adam's action. And yet in 5:14b ("the type of the one who was to come") there is a ray of hope in the comment that Christ — the second Adam — is the bearer of a different fate.

The results of Adam's sin and Christ's death are different (5:15-16). Adam's sin brought sin and death "for many" (= all), whereas Christ's sacrificial death on the cross was the source of God's superabundant grace for all. God's gift is more powerful and more abundant than even sin and death are. Whereas after Adam's sin there was judgment and condemnation (see Gn 3:14-19), Christ's fidelity resulted in justification (acquittal) despite the many sins since Adam.

In 5:17 the difference between Adam and Christ is highlighted with reference to death and life. Adam's sin initiated the reign of death, whereas Christ's fidelity brought about the reign of life that flows from God's grace and justification.

In 5:18-19 the contrasting results are treated with respect to sin and justification. Adam's sin brought condemnation for all, whereas Christ's "righteous act" brought justification and life. Adam's disobedience made sinners of all humans, while Christ's obedience made right relationship with God (justification) a possibility for all.

According to 5:20-21, the Mosaic Law paradoxically added to sin's power (by specifying sins and attracting humans to commit them). Despite the increase of sin, however, Christ's death inaugurated the superabundant reign of grace with its gifts of justification and eternal life.

For Meditation: Adam and Christ are bearers of contrasting fates for all humans. But the gift is not like the transgression. Adam's sin brought disobedience, sin, condemnation, and death. Christ's sacrificial fidelity brought obedience, righteousness, justification/acquittal, and life. The result of Adam's sin was the reign of sin, death, and the Law. The result of Christ's saving death is the reign of grace and life for all humankind. Do you experience the destinies of both Adam and Christ in your own life?

Freedom from the Power of Sin and Death (6:1-11)

[1] What then shall we say? Shall we persist in sin that grace may abound? Of course not!

[2] How can we who died to sin yet live in it? [3] Or are you unaware that we who were baptized into Christ Jesus were baptized into his death? [4] We were indeed buried with him through baptism into death, so that, just as Christ was raised from the dead by the glory of the Father, we too might live in newness of life.

[5] For if we have grown into union with him through a death like his, we shall also be united with him in the resurrection. [6] We know that our old self was crucified with him, so that our sinful body might be done away with, that we might no longer be in slavery to sin. [7] For a dead person has been absolved from sin.

⁸If, then, we have died with Christ, we believe that we shall also live with him. ⁹We know that Christ, raised from the dead, dies no more; death no longer has power over him. ¹⁰As to his death, he died to sin once and for all; as to his life, he lives for God. ¹¹Consequently, you too must think of yourselves as being dead to sin and living for God in Christ Jesus.

Paul's starting point in 6:1-11 is the slanderous accusation made against his gospel of freedom that one should continue in sin so that grace might abound even more. He raised the charge in 3:5-8 but broke off the conversation without really answering it. Here his full answer comes in three parallel sections (6:2-4, 5-7, 8-11) and develops the idea of baptism as our way of sharing the fate or destiny of Christ. Baptism involves a break with the past (life under the power of sin and death) and entrance into the new life of the Holy Spirit. Sin and grace are opposites. To imagine that continuing in sin might promote the life of grace is monstrous. And so Paul in 6:1 answers the accusation quite decisively: "Of course not!"

The first part of the full answer (6:2-4) emphasizes the contradiction between dying to sin in baptism and still living under sin's power. Of all that we would like to know about early Christian baptism, Paul tells us only one (very important) thing. Baptism in Christ Jesus means participating in his action (death and resurrection) and in his fate (life with God). That means freedom from the power of sin, since our lord is no longer sin but now is Christ. Baptism also involves a share in Christ's resurrection, and so we are empowered now to "live in newness of life" — to act in a way that is appropriate to Christians whose full resurrection is in the future but whose behavior in the present serves as a witness and an anticipation of even fuller incorporation into Christ.

The second part (6:5-7) repeats and clarifies the argument, with special emphasis on freedom from the power of sin. The basic point is again that union with Christ's death and resurrection in baptism (6:5) has brought about a change of lords from sin to Christ. This baptism means the end of the "old self" (the Adam in each of us), the "sinful body" (the self under sin's lordship), and "slavery to sin" (taking sin as one's lord). Just as a dead person is absolved from debts at death, so one who has died with Christ in baptism is no longer under obligation to sin.

The emphasis in the third part (6:8-11) is on freedom from the power of death. According to Genesis 3:19, death is the consequence of sin. But sharing in the death of the new Adam means sharing in the life of the risen Christ. Since the risen Christ dies no more and death has no power over him, those who are baptized into Christ already share his freedom and life. Participating in Christ's death and resurrection through baptism demands that we too regard ourselves as "dead to sin and living for God in Christ Jesus" (6:11).

For Meditation: In baptism we have entered into the death of Christ (water as a symbol of death) and into the life of the risen Christ (water as a symbol of life). The new life is the life of the gospel of Jesus Christ. The challenge facing us is to live in a manner that is appropriate to our dignity as persons baptized into Christ. Do you ever make the connection between your baptism and your spirituality?

Freed for Obedience to God (6:12-23)

[12] Therefore, sin must not reign over your mortal bodies so that you obey their desires. [13] And do not present the parts of your bodies to sin as weapons for wickedness, but present yourselves to God as raised from the dead to life and the parts of your bodies to God as weapons for righteousness. [14] For sin is not to have any power over you, since you are not under the law but under grace.

[15] What then? Shall we sin because we are not under the law but under grace? Of course not! [16] Do you not know that if you present yourselves to someone as obedient slaves, you are slaves of the one you obey, either of sin, which leads to death, or of obedience, which leads to righteousness? [17] But thanks be to God that, although you were once slaves of sin, you have become obedient from the heart to the pattern of teaching to which you were entrusted. [18] Freed from sin, you have become slaves of righteousness. [19] I am speaking in human terms because of the weakness of your nature. For just as you presented the parts of your bodies as slaves to impurity and to lawlessness for lawlessness, so now present them as slaves to righteousness for sanctification. [20] For when you were slaves of sin, you were free from righteousness. [21] But what profit did you get then from the things of which you are now

ashamed? For the end of those things is death. [22] But now that you have been freed from sin and have become slaves of God, the benefit that you have leads to sanctification, and its end is eternal life. [23] For the wages of sin is death, but the gift of God is eternal life in Christ Jesus our Lord.

Having been freed from the lordship of sin and death in baptism, and having put on Christ as Lord, Christians are freed for a life of obedience to God. For Paul, freedom is not merely emancipation, autonomy, choice, or free will. Rather, it consists in serving the true Master.

The exhortation in 6:12-14 reflects on the ethical consequences of living for God in the present. Although Christ has broken the ultimate power of sin, one can still experience sin's power. And so in 6:12-13 Paul urges Christians not to allow sin to have mastery over them. The image of "mortal bodies" (that is, subject to death) in 6:12 reinforces the link between sin and death. The military imagery in 6:13 highlights the opposition between life under sin ("weapons for wickedness") and life under Christ ("weapons for righteousness"). In 6:14 Paul explains that over those who live "under grace" and not "under the law" sin should have no dominion. Accepting the lordship of Christ means rejecting sin, death, and the Law as lords over one's life.

In 6:15 Paul returns to the accusation raised in 6:1 (and 3:5-8) that, according to Paul's gospel, being under grace allows one to sin. Again Paul's immediate response is a decisive "Of course not!"

As Paul develops his answer in 6:16-23, Paul invokes a series of sharp contrasts between life under sin and the newness of life in Christ: "under the law" versus "under grace" (6:15), "sin" and "death" versus "obedience" and "righteousness" (6:16), "slaves of sin" versus "obedient to the pattern of teaching" (6:17), "sin" versus "righteousness" (6:18, 20), "impurity" and "lawlessness" versus "righteousness" and "sanctification" (6:19), and "death" versus "eternal life" (6:21-23).

Each pair makes the same basic point, and one could take almost any sentence as a summary of the whole exhortation. One good example appears in 6:18: "Freed from sin, you have become slaves of righteousness." It is customary to describe the core of Paul's ethical teaching as the convergence of the imperative and the indicative ("Become what you are!"). Accepting the lordship of Christ means acting in a manner that befits one's baptismal identity "in Christ." It means obedient service of the new Lord and the rejection of everything that counts as sin.

For Meditation: In Paul's contrasts between life under sin and life under Christ, there are few "grays." It is usually "either . . . or" rather than "both . . . and." And yet 6:12-14 suggests the possibility that someone under Christ might slip back into being under sin. Paul's ethical teaching does not stand on its own as prudent or practical advice. Rather, it flows from Paul's theological interpretation of the human situation in the light of Christ. How does Paul's understanding of

71

freedom as the obedient service of God compare with popular ideas about freedom today?

Freed from the Law (7:1-6)

[1] Are you unaware, brothers (for I am speaking to you as people who know the law), that the law has jurisdiction over one as long as one lives? [2] Thus a married woman is bound by law to her living husband; but if her husband dies, she is released from the law in respect to her husband. [3] Consequently, while her husband is alive she will be called an adulteress if she consorts with another man. But if her husband dies she is free from that law, and she is not an adulteress if she consorts with another man.

[4] In the same way, my brothers, you also were put to death to the law through the body of Christ, so that you might belong to another, to the one who was raised from the dead in order that we might bear fruit for God. [5] For when we were in the flesh, our sinful passions, awakened by the law, worked in our members to bear fruit for death. [6] But now we are released from the law, dead to what held us captive, so that we may serve in the newness of the spirit and not under the obsolete letter.

Although Paul sometimes interprets the Mosaic Law positively as a witness to Christ (see 3:21), he also sometimes views it negatively as an ally of sin and death. From his pastoral activity among Gentile Christians, Paul was convinced that such persons did not have to become Jews in order to be good Christians. He contended that what God has done in Christ was sufficient to make possible for them right relationship with God apart from their observing the Mosaic Law. Though Paul seems to have had no objection to Jewish Christians observing precepts of the Law, he did argue vehemently against Jewish Christians and other Jews who might make the Law into the means of their justification on a par with Christ. His problem was not so much with the Law itself (see 7:12) but with those who would make it equal or superior to Christ.

In 7:1 Paul introduces his reflections on freedom from the Law by invoking the legal principle that the law (here law in general rather than the Mosaic Law) has force only over those who are alive. Then to illustrate the principle, he develops in 7:2-3 an analogy about a married woman. While her husband lives, she is bound by certain laws. When he dies, however, she is released from all legal obligations to her husband. For her to consort with another man during her husband's lifetime is adultery from a legal perspective. But after her husband's death, the same action is not adultery (assuming the man is free too). The point of the analogy is that death changes one's relation to law.

In 7:4-6 Paul argues for freedom from the Mosaic Law in the light of many themes from chapter 6. His basic principle is that death absolves one from otherwise binding legal obligations. Since baptism is a kind of death that frees one from the lordship of sin and death and effects participation in Christ's death and resurrection, it also marks "death to the law" (7:4) as the ally of sin of death. In 7:5 Paul describes how sin, death, and the Mosaic Law worked together: When we were under sin's lordship ("in the flesh"), the Law aroused sinful passions (by specifying sins and tempting us to commit them) and led to sins whose result was death. In 7:6 Paul takes the reflection in a more positive direction. The goal of freedom from the Mosaic Law is to serve God "in the newness of the spirit" (the same word may refer both to the opposite of the "flesh" and to the Holy Spirit). When the Mosaic Law is taken as the equal of Christ and as the means of right relationship with God, it is aptly described as "what held us captive" and as "the obsolete letter." In this perspective, Gentile Christians need not observe the Mosaic Law, nor should Jewish Christians forget its limitations.

For Meditation: Although Paul begins in 7:1-3 by talking about law in general, in 7:4-6 he focuses on the Law of Moses as an ally of sin and death. The later distinction between the moral and cultic teachings of the Law—with only the moral precepts still in force— seems unknown to Paul. Paul's fundamental problem with the Law is that it is not on the same level as Christ, and it cannot do what Christ did. He is on guard against any who would reduce Christ to the level of the Law, and he goes so far as to link it with sin and death. In what sense is freedom from the Law positive teaching?

Sin and the Law (7:7-11)

⁷What then can we say? That the law is sin? Of course not! Yet I did not know sin except through the law, and I did not know what it is to covet except

that the law said, "You shall not covet." [8]But sin, finding an opportunity in the commandment, produced in me every kind of covetousness. Apart from the law sin is dead. [9]I once lived outside the law, but when the commandment came, sin became alive; [10]then I died, and the commandment that was for life turned out to be death for me. [11]For sin, seizing an opportunity in the commandment, deceived me and through it put me to death.

How the Law worked as an ally of sin (see 7:5) is described in more detail in 7:7-11. The main problem of interpretation in the passage is the identity of the "I." It is probably not strictly autobiographical, since Paul did not live "outside" the Law (7:9) before his conversion to Christ (see Phil 3:5-6). It is probably to be taken as describing typical human experience (Adam's experience and ours) both under and before the Law. Insofar as Paul shared that experience, it is also personal testimony. But it need not be taken as evidence for Paul having been a particularly scrupulous or tortured soul. Compare his claim in Philippians 3:6: "In righteousness based on the law I was blameless."

After denying that the Law itself is sin and was intended as such, Paul describes the experience of one who is under the Mosaic Law. In 7:7 he claims that "I" (as one under the Law) came to know what sin is through the Law and in particular learned how to covet or desire (see Ex 20:17; Dt 5:21), which is the beginning of all sin. Thus the Mosaic Law served as a stimulus to sin and gave power and life to sin (7:8).

In 7:9-11 Paul describes the experience of one who lived before the giving of the Law; that is, from Adam to Moses. In fact, we have to see Adam as the main character here, since there is nothing that does not apply to Adam, and only to Adam does everything apply. Adam lived not only outside the Mosaic Law but apart from any divine command before Genesis 2:16-17. But when the divine command not to eat from the tree of knowledge of good and bad came to Adam from God (Gn 2:17), sin took on a life of its own and the result was death for Adam and for all humankind (see Gn 3:19). Whereas God's command was intended to reveal the divine will to Adam, the consequence was that the command awakened the whole process of sin in Adam and led to death. Even though Adam did not yet have the whole Mosaic Law, his sinful response to the divine command illustrates the dynamic that the Law introduced. Thus, according to 7:11, the command provided an opportunity for sin and brought death rather than the life that the serpent promised (see Gn 3:5).

For Meditation: Whether under the entire Mosaic Law or merely under the single command given to Adam, humans risk the possibility of perverting the divine will and so falling into the process of sin that merits death. Here Paul is adding to his case that the Law cannot be regarded as the equal of Christ by focusing on its negative side — bringing knowledge of sin and thus serving as sin's instrument. Have you ever experienced the process that Paul describes in this passage?

Life Under Sin and the Law (7:12-25)

¹²So then the law is holy, and the commandment is holy and righteous and good. ¹³Did the good, then, become death for me? Of course not! Sin, in order that it might be shown to be sin, worked death in me through the good, so that sin might become sinful beyond measure through the commandment.

¹⁴We know that the law is spiritual; but I am carnal, sold into slavery to sin. ¹⁵What I do, I do not understand. For I do not do what I want, but I do what I hate. ¹⁶Now if I do what I do not want, I concur that the law is good. ¹⁷So it is no longer I who do it, but sin that dwells in me. ¹⁸For I know that good does not dwell in me, that is, in my flesh. The willing is ready at hand, but doing the good is not. ¹⁹For I do not do the good I want, but I do the evil I do not want. ²⁰Now if I do what I do not want, it is no longer I who do it, but sin that dwells in me.

²¹So, then, I discover the principle that when I want to do right, evil is at hand. ²²For I take delight in the law of God, in my inner self, ²³but I see in my members another principle at war with the law of my mind, taking me captive to the law of sin that dwells in my members.

²⁴Miserable one that I am! Who will deliver me from this mortal body? ²⁵Thanks be to God through Jesus Christ our Lord. Therefore, I myself, with my mind, serve the law of God but, with my flesh, the law of sin.

Paul continues his reflection on human existence ("I") under and before the Law. Having taken his criticism of the Law about as far as possible without denying its divine origin, he affirms in 7:12 that the

Mosaic Law is indeed "holy," and that the commandment (probably God's command to Adam) is "holy and righteous and good." But once more taking the role of Adam and Adam's descendants, Paul in 7:13 shows how sin used the good command to "become sinful beyond measure" and so to work further death.

In 7:14-18 Paul describes what it is to live under the power of sin. Such a one is "carnal" or "fleshly," and so is sold into slavery with sin as the master (7:14). The result is the divided self that knows and wills the good but fails to do it (7:15-16). In such a person sin has taken up residence as a master and works through the "I" (7:17). The aspect of the human person that makes possible such domination by sin is the "flesh" — a term that describes the person as fallen away and estranged from God (7:18). In 7:19-20 Paul once more presents what it means to be possessed by the power of sin: The evil that "I" do not want to do is what "I" do — because sin dwells in me.

The topic of the divided self is further explored in 7:21-23. The human person under and before the Law is in the middle of a war. The combatants are the desire in the "inner self" to follow God's law (the natural law and the Torah) and sin, which has a dominion over the person that results in evil actions and death. Paul's teaching here is like the Jewish idea of the good and the evil inclinations at war in the individual. The chief difference is in Paul's personification of sin as an alien force taking up residence in the person.

The reflection ends with a lament ("Miserable one that I am!") and a question ("Who will deliver me. . .?"). The expression "mortal body" in 7:24 aptly describes what Paul has been discussing throughout the chapter: Where sin dwells, death characterizes human existence. Paul knows very well that the answer to his own question is Christ, and so he anticipates in 7:25a the positive picture of life in the Spirit that he will give in chapter 8. But before that, he gives in 7:25b one last picture of the divided self that serves God's law with the "mind" but serves sin with the "flesh."

For Meditation: Paul's analysis of human existence under and before the Law is intended to show once more the absolute need for Christ ("Who will deliver me. . .?"). One partial analogy to what Paul describes here is the experience of addiction (to alcohol, drugs, or something else) that can drive people to do what they really do not want to do, and that can alienate them not only from their loved ones but even from themselves. To what extent does the addiction analogy help you to understand this text, and where does it fall short?

V

The Gospel and Life in the Spirit

The gospel frees us for life in the Holy Spirit, to live in the "spirit" rather than in the "flesh." Romans 8 is arguably the most important chapter in the entire letter, which is arguably the most important book in the Bible. After describing how the Holy Spirit empowers us to live in the spirit (8:1-11), Paul establishes our identity as children of God (8:12-17), reflects on the present-future and individual-cosmic dimensions of Christian spirituality (8:18-25), presents some surprising and profound teachings about prayer (8:26-27), and grounds and develops the affirmation that God is for us and with us (8:28-39). All this is what the event celebrated in the gospel enables one to be and do.

Life in the Spirit (8:1-11)

¹ Hence, now there is no condemnation for those who are in Christ Jesus. ² For the law of the spirit of life in Christ Jesus has freed you from the law of sin and death. ³ For what the law, weakened by the flesh, was powerless to do, this God has done: by sending his own Son in the likeness of sinful flesh and for the sake of sin, he condemned sin in the flesh, ⁴ so that the righteous decree of the law might be fulfilled

in us, who live not according to the flesh but according to the spirit.

⁵For those who live according to the flesh are concerned with the things of the flesh, but those who live according to the spirit with the things of the spirit. ⁶The concern of the flesh is death, but the concern of the spirit is life and peace. ⁷For the concern of the flesh is hostility toward God: it does not submit to the law of God, nor can it; ⁸and those who are in the flesh cannot please God.

⁹But you are not in the flesh; on the contrary, you are in the spirit, if only the Spirit of God dwells in you. Whoever does not have the Spirit of Christ does not belong to him. ¹⁰But if Christ is in you, although the body is dead because of sin, the spirit is alive because of righteousness. ¹¹If the Spirit of the one who raised Jesus from the dead dwells in you, the one who raised Jesus from the dead will give life to your mortal bodies also, through his Spirit that dwells in you.

The Greek word *pneuma* can refer to the Holy "Spirit" as well as to the "spirit" as the aspect of the person that is open and responsive to God. At some points in Romans 8 it is difficult to know which is meant, and perhaps sometimes both are intended. In 8:1-11 Paul provides the foundation of Christian spirituality by explaining how the Holy Spirit makes it possible to live in the spirit.

Much of what was said about freedom from sin, death, and the Law in chapters 5–7 is summarized in 8:1-4. Since justification has already taken place for those who are "in Christ" (see 5:9, 18), they have no need to fear "condemnation" at the last judgment. In

8:2-4 Paul shifts the meanings of *nomos* between its general sense of "principle" and its specific meaning as the Mosaic Law. What the Mosaic Law could not achieve (freedom from the power of sin and death), God has done in Christ Jesus (8:2). The proper answer to Paul's question in 7:24 ("Who will deliver me. . .?") is "the law of the spirit of life in Christ Jesus." The opposite of "spirit" is "flesh" — the aspect of the human person that is closed and hostile to God. Those who live under the dominion of sin, death, and the Law are in the flesh. Rather than extricating humans from the flesh, the Law added to their enslavement. But God, by sending his Son Jesus (8:3; see Gal 4:4; Phil 2:6-11; Jn 3:16-17; 1 Jn 4:9) as a human being ("in the likeness of sinful flesh"), overcame the power of sin. As a result, what the Law really intended ("the righteous decree of the law") is now fulfilled among those who live according to the spirit (8:4).

The opposition between flesh and spirit is further developed in 8:5-8, where Paul explains what being in the flesh means. Those who live in the flesh set their minds on things of the flesh which lead to death, whereas those who live in the spirit set their minds on things of the spirit which lead to life and peace (8:5-6). Life in the flesh involves rebellion against God, disobedience toward God's law, and failure to please God (8:7-8).

In 8:9-11 Paul explains what being in the spirit/Spirit means. Just as sin takes up residence in those who live according to the flesh (see 7:17), so the Holy Spirit takes up residence in those who live according to the spirit. Those who are in Christ have the Spirit of God dwelling in them (8:9). In 8:9-11 the Holy Spirit is given several different names: "the Spirit of God," "the Spirit of Christ," "the Spirit of the one who raised Jesus from the death," and "his Spirit." All three persons of the Trinity share in the work of justification and sanctification through God's Spirit. The Spirit enables us to share the life of the risen Christ.

For Meditation: Christian spirituality proceeds from the initiative of the Holy Spirit. It is first and foremost a response to the action of God's Holy Spirit in our lives. The initiative of the Holy Spirit in turn empowers us to live in the realm of the spirit rather than the realm of the flesh. Where do you live your life, and whose direction do you follow?

Children of God (8:12-17)

¹²Consequently, brothers, we are not debtors to the flesh, to live according to the flesh. ¹³For if you live according to the flesh, you will die, but if by the spirit you put to death the deeds of the body, you will live.

¹⁴For those who are led by the Spirit of God are children of God. ¹⁵For you did not receive a spirit of slavery to fall back into fear, but you received a spirit of adoption, through which we cry, *Abba*, "Father!"

¹⁶The Spirit itself bears witness with our spirit that we are children of God, ¹⁷and if children, then heirs, heirs of God and joint heirs with Christ, if only

we suffer with him, so that we may also be glorified with him.

In 8:12-13 Paul recapitulates his teaching about the opposition between "flesh" and "spirit." Those who live under the flesh ("debtors to the flesh") end in death, whereas those who live under the spirit will live. Life in the spirit demands not only reception of the Holy Spirit's initiative but also the commitment to live one's life in the spirit by facing up to the challenges and temptations of human existence.

Those who are directed or guided by God's Spirit are "children of God" (8:14). The new relationship with God that has been created by the Spirit of Christ is one of parent-child rather than of master-slave. In 8:15 Paul uses the figure of "adoption" to describe how those who are led by the Spirit have become full members of God's family. Under Adam's sin we were alienated from God and at best slaves or servants of God. But through Christ's death and resurrection we can enjoy a relationship of intimacy with God, and so approach God with the trust and reverence that a child brings to a loving parent. We can approach God as Jesus did and taught us to do — as *Abba* ("Father"). The Aramaic word *Abba* has been taken over into Hebrew (and New Testament Greek). It is how small children address their parent, and how we now can address God.

According to 8:16, those who live in the spirit and under the Spirit's leadership know that they are children of God. As true (adopted) children of God they share with God's Son Jesus the rights and privileges of God's children: "heirs of God and joint heirs with Christ" (8:17a). In 8:17b, however, Paul deflects what could be a triumphalistic train of thought by observing that being God's children along with Jesus involves suffering ("if only we suffer with him"). Only one who shares Christ's passion can share the risen Christ's glory (see 6:3-4).

For Meditation: Those who live in the spirit under the Spirit's direction are true children of God and have Jesus as their brother. They constitute the family of God. Of course, not everyone has loving parents or an intact and well-functioning family. And so this imagery may be hard for some. Those blessed with a positive family experience may find helpful the idea of being part of God's family with Christ. Those not so blessed can at least project an ideal family and profit also from the imagery. Does the image of being God's children with Christ in the Spirit help you to appreciate what God has done for us and to live your life in a positive manner?

Waiting in Hope (8:18-25)

[18] I consider that the sufferings of this present time are as nothing compared with the glory to be revealed for us. [19] For creation awaits with eager expectation the revelation of the children of God; [20] for creation was made subject to futility, not of its own accord but because of the one who subjected it, in hope [21] that creation itself would be set free from

85

slavery to corruption and share in the glorious freedom of the children of God.

[22] We know that all creation is groaning in labor pains even until now; [23] and not only that, but we ourselves, who have the firstfruits of the Spirit, we also groan within ourselves as we wait for adoption, the redemption of our bodies. [24] For in hope we were saved. Now hope that sees for itself is not hope. For who hopes for what one sees? [25] But if we hope for what we do not see, we wait with endurance.

For Paul, having the Spirit and waiting for the fullness of God's kingdom coincide. In 8:18 Paul acknowledges again the reality of human suffering (see 5:3-5; 8:17) but regards it as not so important in relation to the coming fullness of God's kingdom ("the glory to be revealed"). The whole of creation, along with humankind, enter into a sympathetic relation of expectation for the fullness of God's kingdom. In the present, creation too stands in a state of "futility" (8:20) and "slavery to corruption" (8:21) that is analogous to the situation of humankind under the power of sin and death (though God remains in ultimate control). Likewise, creation too will share the glorious freedom that God's children will enjoy on the Day of the Lord.

The same point is made again in 8:22-23. The "groaning in labor pains" (8:22) that creation experiences is parallel to the groaning even of those who now have the gift of the Spirit but long for its fullness. The gift of the Spirit in the present is described as the "firstfruits" — the earliest part of a harvest but not its complete yield. The situation in which those who live in the spirit under God's Spirit is hope. The proper object of hope is what we do not yet see (8:24-25), and so the attitude of the confident believer during the present is patient and hope-filled "endurance."

For Meditation: The gift of the Holy Spirit is the basis of Christian spirituality in the present. As Christians, we also await in hope the future glory that is to be revealed with the fullness of God's kingdom. Moreover, Christian spirituality involves us not only as individuals but also as part of humankind and indeed of the whole created universe that eagerly awaits with us the definitive revelation of God's glory. Christian spirituality has present and future, as well as individual, social, and cosmic dimensions. What place do these various dimensions actually have in your spirituality?

The Spirit and Prayer (8:26-27)

26 In the same way, the Spirit too comes to the aid of our weakness; for we do not know how to pray as we ought, but the Spirit itself intercedes with inexpressible groanings. 27 And the one who searches hearts knows what is the intention of the Spirit, because it intercedes for the holy ones according to God's will.

An essential element of life in the spirit under God's Spirit is prayer. In 8:26-27 Paul considers the Holy Spirit's role in prayer. The starting point is the acknowledgment of human weakness before God. The Holy Spirit helps us to express what we want to say to God even when the best we can do is groan or sigh (8:26). The Holy Spirit also helps God ("the one who searches hearts") to understand what we say in prayer (8:27). The Holy Spirit makes sure that our prayers (however inadequate they may seem) are heard and properly interpreted by God.

For Meditation: According to Paul, the Holy Spirit is the principal agent in prayer, and we in our human weakness cooperate with the Holy Spirit. Prayer is not something that we do entirely on our own. Rather, prayer is something that the Holy Spirit does through us. What impact might this insight about prayer have upon your approach to and practice of prayer?

God is For Us (8:28-39)

[28] We know that all things work for good for those who love God, who are called according to his purpose. [29] For those he foreknew he also predestined to be conformed to the image of his Son, so that he might be the firstborn among many brothers. [30] And those he predestined he also called; and those he called he also justified; and those he justified he also glorified.

[31] What then shall we say to this? If God is for us, who can be against us? [32] He who did not spare his own Son but handed him over for us all, how will he not also give us everything else along with him? [33] Who will bring a charge against God's chosen ones? It is God who acquits us. [34] Who will con-

demn? It is Christ Jesus who died, rather, was raised, who also is at the right hand of God, who intercedes for us.

³⁵ What will separate us from the love of Christ? Will anguish, or distress, or persecution, or famine, or nakedness, or peril, or the sword? ³⁶ As it is written: "For your sake we are being slain all the day; we are looked upon as sheep to be slaughtered." ³⁷ No, in all these things we conquer overwhelmingly through him who loved us. ³⁸ For I am convinced that neither death, nor life, nor angels, nor principalities, nor present things, nor future things, nor powers, ³⁹ nor height, nor depth, nor any other creature will be able to separate us from the love of God in Christ Jesus our Lord.

The fundamental conviction of Christian spirituality according to Paul is that God is for us and with us. The assertion in 8:28 that "all things work for good for those who love God" is no guarantee of success in all endeavors (the "success gospel"). In fact, "all things" most likely refers to the sufferings endured in the present (see 8:18). The claim is that God can and does draw good results from what seem to be negative experiences.

The five verbs in 8:29-30 ("foreknew . . . predestined . . . called . . . justified . . . glorified") describe God's initiative in the full range of the spiritual life. The first three verbs highlight God's special care for us before we do anything at all. The term "justified" expresses the right relationship with God that has been made possible through Jesus' death and resurrection, while the word "glorified" points to fullness of life with

God — the future state, eternal happiness, and life in God's kingdom. God is for us and with us from start to finish. What God makes of us is well expressed in passing in 8:29b: "conformed to the image of his Son, so that he might be the firstborn among many brothers." Being "conformed" to Christ is the essence of Christian spirituality (see Phil 3:10).

The decisive proof that God is for us is found in Jesus' death "for us all" (8:32). The statement that "God did not spare his own Son" evokes Abraham's willingness to sacrifice his son Isaac (Gn 22:16). The imaginative context of these affirmations about God and Christ is the law court. Since God is for us (8:31), we need not fear opposition. Since God is our defender, no one can bring a charge against "God's chosen ones" and expect to prevail (8:33). Since Christ is the judge, no one can condemn those who are "in Christ" (8:34). Indeed, the risen Christ intercedes for us with God in the heavenly court just as the Holy Spirit intercedes for us on earth (see 8:26-27).

The concluding section (8:35-39) is more celebratory than didactic. Having reflected on various aspects of life in the Spirit, Paul breaks into an emotional shout: "What will separate us from the love of Christ?" The obvious answer is, no one and no thing. The "love of Christ" refers first of all to the love that Christ has shown for us in his passion and death. It also refers to the love that we have for Christ in return. Not even the worst and most difficult experiences that humans undergo ("anguish . . . the sword") can separate us (8:35). Neither can superhuman forces ("death . . .

any other creature") separate us from the love that God has shown to us in Christ or from the love we have for Christ (8:38-39). Since God has made us conquerors (over sin and death) through Christ, we can live with the confidence that God is really for us and with us.

For Meditation: The fundamental conviction of Christian spirituality is that God is for us and with us. God initiates the relationship. God is with us from start to finish. What we do is a response to God's love for us. Do you really trust God?

VI

The Gospel and God's Plan

Thus far Paul has explained how Gentiles can be part of God's people — by faith after the pattern of Abraham and Christ. But if the gospel really is such a great gift from God, why had so many Jews not embraced it? Of course, Paul and other early Christians were Jews by birth. However, they hardly constituted a majority within Judaism. In Romans 9–11 Paul reflects on the relationships in God's plan among Jewish Christians, Gentile Christians, and Jews who do not accept the gospel. He argues that each group has an indispensable role in salvation history.

Romans 9–11 is an important part of Paul's letter to the Romans. It should not be passed over because of its difficult logic and sometimes strained biblical interpretations. Rather, it is an opportunity to share Paul's wonder and excitement at what he perceived to be the unfolding of God's plan and the central place of the gospel within it. It also served as the basis for much of what is said in Vatican II's *Nostra Aetate* 4 about the relationship of the Church to the Jewish people today. For those concerned with Christian-Jewish relations, Romans 9–11 is the most important text in the entire New Testament.

Paul's Lament and Israel's Privileges (9:1-5)

¹I speak the truth in Christ, I do not lie; my conscience joins with the Holy Spirit in bearing me witness ²that I have great sorrow and constant anguish in my heart. ³For I could wish that I myself were accursed and separated from Christ for the sake of my brothers, my kin according to the flesh.

⁴They are Israelites; theirs the adoption, the glory, the covenants, the giving of the law, the worship, and the promises; ⁵theirs the patriarchs, and from them, according to the flesh, is the Messiah. God who is over all be blessed forever. Amen.

Paul was convinced that Jesus' death and resurrection fulfilled God's promises to Israel and was the climax of the history of Israel. Some Jews agreed, but most did not. And so Paul had to deal with the reality that many Jews did not see God's plan unfolding as Paul did.

How deeply disappointed Paul felt can be sensed from his lament in 9:1-3. Continuing the courtroom imagery from 8:31-34, he first protests his truthfulness and invokes both his conscience and the Holy Spirit as witnesses (9:1). Then in 9:2 he confesses how painful ("great sorrow and constant anguish in my heart") the Jewish rejection of Jesus was for him. In 9:3 he even claims that he went so far as to pray to be cut off (*anathema*) from Christ if it would help his fellow Jews to accept the gospel. Identification with Christ was the most important thing in Paul's life — as Romans 1–8 demonstrates. And yet, so deeply did

Paul feel about his fellow Jews that he would have been willing to forgo that on their behalf.

Having expressed his personal involvement in the matter that he will treat throughout chapters 9–11, Paul in 9:4-5 lists the privileges of Israel as God's people and in God's plan. There is no grammatical warrant for putting these privileges in the past tense ("theirs were"), and indeed in 11:29 Paul states that God's gifts and call to Israel are irrevocable. The privileges included adoption by God (see Ex 4:22, "Israel is my son, my firstborn"), the glory (God's presence in the wilderness and in the Jerusalem temple), the covenants (with Abraham, Moses, David, etc.), the giving of the Law (on Mount Sinai), the worship (chiefly temple sacrifices), the promises (of God's fidelity to Israel), the patriarchs (Abraham, Isaac, Jacob, Moses, etc.), and the Messiah (Jesus of Nazareth). These privileges are the premise of the meditation that follows, and so Paul seals the list with a benediction ("God who is over all be blessed forever. Amen").

For Meditation: By expressing his willingness to be cut off from Christ on behalf of his fellow Jews, Paul emphasizes how important he considered the Jewish rejection of Jesus to be. His sorrow was increased by the recognition of historic Israel's privileges in salvation history, especially since Jesus the Messiah came from Israel and, according to Paul, fulfilled God's promises to Israel. How do you assess Paul's statements in 9:3 — as a genuine offer or as rhetorical overstatement?

The Surprising Way of God (9:6-13)

> ⁶But it is not that the word of God has failed. For not all who are of Israel are Israel, ⁷nor are they all children of Abraham because they are his descendants; but "It is through Isaac that descendants shall bear your name." ⁸This means that it is not the children of the flesh who are the children of God, but the children of the promise are counted as descendants. ⁹For this is the wording of the promise, "About this time I shall return and Sarah will have a son."
>
> ¹⁰And not only that, but also when Rebecca had conceived children by one husband, our father Isaac — ¹¹before they had yet been born or had done anything, good or bad, in order that God's elective plan might continue, ¹²not by works but by his call — she was told, "The older shall serve the younger." ¹³As it is written: "I loved Jacob but hated Esau."

Paul's major concern in Romans 9–11 was to show that "it is not that the word of God has failed" (9:6a). And so he tried to demonstrate from the Jewish Scriptures ("the word of God") that what God was doing with Jewish Christians, Gentile Christians, and non-Christian Jews was in accord with God's surprising way of acting. In other words, what God did in and through Christ was consistent with the way in which God had acted throughout the history of salvation.

In 9:6b-9 Paul shows from the example of Abraham and Isaac that merely belonging to ethnic Israel is no guarantee of being part of God's people. It is not simply a matter of claiming physical descent from Abraham (see Rom 4). According to Genesis 25:1-18,

Abraham had other children by his wives Keturah and Hagar (notably Ishmael). Nevertheless, it was only through Isaac, the child of Sarah, that God's promise to Abraham (see Gn 18:10, 14) was fulfilled. Thus God defined Israel not in terms of the "flesh" but of the "promise" (9:8). According to the Scriptures, therefore, not everyone who is a physical child of Abraham is automatically a recipient of God's promises to Israel. This helps Paul to explain why Gentiles could be children of Abraham and why not all Jews were accepting the gospel.

A second biblical example — the birth of Esau and Jacob to Rebecca and Isaac (see Gn 25:19-34) — shows again that God has always worked on the basis of his sovereign will and not mere physical descent. Even though Esau and Jacob were twins and Esau in fact was slightly older, God chose Jacob as the vehicle for fulfilling the promise to Abraham (see Gn 25:33; Mal 1:2-3). Again, it was a matter of God's sovereign will, not one of human rights and works.

For Meditation: By invoking the biblical examples of Isaac and Jacob, Paul seeks to establish the pattern of God's activity with humankind in general and with God's people in particular. God works in the realm of election and promise, not that of claims to physical descent and human achievements. The results are often surprising — just as the inclusion of Gentiles among God's people through Christ and the refusal by many Jews to embrace the gospel were. Have you experienced the surprising ways of God in your life?

God's Sovereign Freedom and Justice (9:14-23)

¹⁴What then are we to say? Is there injustice on the part of God? Of course not! ¹⁵For he says to Moses: "I will show mercy to whom I will, I will take pity on whom I will." ¹⁶So it depends not upon a person's will or exertion, but upon God, who shows mercy. ¹⁷For the Scripture says to Pharaoh, "This is why I have raised you up, to show my power through you that my name may be proclaimed throughout the earth." ¹⁸Consequently, he has mercy upon whom he wills, and he hardens whom he wills.

¹⁹You will say to me then, "Why then does he still find fault? For who can oppose his will?" ²⁰But who indeed are you, a human being, to talk back to God? Will what is made say to its maker, "Why have you created me so?" ²¹Or does not the potter have a right over the clay, to make out of the same lump one vessel for a noble purpose and another for an ignoble one?

²²What if God, wishing to show his wrath and make known his power, has endured with much patience the vessels of wrath made for destruction? ²³This was to make known the riches of his glory to the vessels of mercy, which he has prepared previously for glory, ²⁴namely, us whom he has called, not only from the Jews but also from the Gentiles.

If God chose Isaac over Ishmael and Jacob over Esau, is God unjust? After a strong initial response to this objection against God's justice ("Of course not!"), Paul in 9:15-18 adds the even more striking example of God's choice of Moses over Pharaoh, the king of Egypt. He first quotes Exodus 33:19 ("I will show mercy . . . on whom I will") and uses it to defend God's sovereign freedom (9:15-16). Then he quotes Exodus 9:16 to suggest that even through Pharaoh and his hardened heart God's purposes were being advanced (9:17-18).

In 9:19 Paul returns to the question raised in 9:14: If everything depends on God's sovereign freedom, how can God condemn those who have not been chosen as the objects of his mercy? Rather than answering that question directly, Paul invokes the familiar image of the potter and the clay. Just as the clay has no right to dictate and complain to the potter, so humans have no right to dictate or complain to God about what God must do with creatures and how they are to be used to further the divine plan. The analogy is not so much an answer as it is a challenge to look at the matter from a divine rather than human perspective.

Picking up on the idea of vessels made for noble and ignoble purposes, Paul in 9:22-24 distinguishes between "the vessels of wrath made for destruction" (such as Pharaoh) and "the vessels of mercy" (such as Isaac, Jacob, and Moses). The latter are said to have been "prepared previously for glory" (9:23). Finally, in 9:24 Paul identifies as present-day "vessels of mercy" both Jewish Christians and Gentile Christians.

For Meditation: The major point here is the sovereign freedom of God in directing human affairs and salvation history. God has always acted in this way (as Lord of history) and continues to do so in forming the Church of Jesus Christ. To accuse God of injustice or to obsess over the fate of the "vessels of wrath" and over the apparent predestination implied by 9:23 is to bring a limited human perspective to these matters. And this is precisely what Paul argues against. Why do you think that some people embrace the gospel and live by it, and others do not?

The Present State of God's People and Scripture (9:25-29)

> 25 As indeed he says in Hosea: "Those who were not my people I will call 'my people,' and her who was not beloved I will call 'beloved.' 26 And in the very place where it was said to them, 'You are not my people,' there they shall be called children of the living God."
>
> 27 And Isaiah cries out concerning Israel, "Though the number of the Israelites were like the sand of the sea, only a remnant will be saved; 28 for decisively and quickly will the Lord execute sentence upon the earth." 29 And as Isaiah predicted: "Unless the Lord of hosts had left us descendants, we would have become like Sodom and have been made like Gomorrah."

The present but provisional goal of salvation history is the Church made up of Jews and Gentiles (9:24). With reference to the biblical prophets Hosea and Isaiah, Paul seeks to show that the present state of the Church is related to God's promises to Israel, and that the Church's inclusion of Gentiles and Jews stands in accord with God's plan revealed in the Scriptures.

The first set of biblical quotations (9:25-26)

grounds the inclusion of non-Jews among God's people in the Church. The key expressions are "not my people" and "not beloved" in Hosea 2:25 and "not my people" in Hosea 2:1. In the book of Hosea these epithets apply to Israel in moral rebellion against God. Paul, however, takes them as references to Gentiles and uses them to defend the inclusion of Gentile Christians in the Church ("beloved" and "children of the living God").

The second set of biblical quotations (9:27-29) explains the presence of only some Jews in the Church. With reference to Isaiah 10:22-23 Paul identifies Jewish Christians like himself as the "remnant" within Israel as opposed to the majority of Israel. Nevertheless, with the help of Isaiah 1:9 he insists that God does not abandon Israel to destruction ("like Sodom . . . like Gomorrah") but preserves Israel through the participation of Jewish Christians like himself in the Church ("left us descendants").

For Meditation: The Church in Paul's time consisted of Gentile and Jewish Christians. The Jewish Scriptures themselves are invoked by Paul to explain and justify why Gentiles are now part of the people of God, and how Jewish Christians as the "remnant" preserve continuity with Israel as the biblical people of God. Paul refuses to cut off the Church from Israel. In what ways does the Church today continue its relation to Israel, and what impact might this link have on your spirituality?

Israel's Mistake (9:30–10:4)

30 What then shall we say? That Gentiles, who did not pursue righteousness, have achieved it, that is, righteousness that comes from faith; 31 but that Israel, who pursued the law of righteousness, did not attain to that law? 32 Why not? Because they did it not by faith, but as if it could be done by works. They stumbled over the stone that causes stumbling, 33 as it is written : "Behold, I am laying a stone in Zion that will make people stumble and a rock that will make them fall, and whoever believes in him shall not be put to shame."

10:1 Brothers, my heart's desire and prayer to God on their behalf is for salvation. 2 I testify with regard to them that they have zeal for God, but it is not discerning. 3 For, in their unawareness of the righteousness that comes from God and their attempt to establish their own righteousness, they did not submit to the righteousness of God. 4 For Christ is the end of the law for the justification of everyone who has faith.

Having explained why Gentiles can be part of God's people and how Jewish Christians carry on the heritage of Israel, Paul now turns to the more difficult task of explaining why much of Israel has not embraced the gospel.

In 9:30-31 Paul contrasts Gentiles who did not pursue righteousness but nonetheless attained it through faith with those in Israel who pursued righteousness but did not succeed in attaining it. The reason is that the latter mistakenly thought that they could achieve right relationship with God through the

Law. Whereas the ignorance of Gentiles was overcome, the misunderstanding of non-Christian Jews was not. Their mistake according to 9:32a was in imagining that the Law was the means of gaining right relationship with God (justification), whereas only faith could make that possible (as the example of Abraham showed). And so Christ became for them a stumbling block (9:32b-33). The combination of Isaiah 28:16 and 8:14 quoted in 9:33 appears also in Matthew 21:42 and 1 Peter 2:6, which suggests that the pairing was already traditional in early Christian circles. Paul uses it to emphasize faith in the gospel of Jesus Christ as what separates those who stumble and fall (non-Christian Jews) and those whom God will vindicate (Jew and Gentile Christians).

In 10:1-2 Paul grows emotional again (see 9:1-3) about his fellow Jews' refusal to accept the gospel and the salvation it brings. He praises their zeal but dismisses it as misplaced. In 10:3 he expresses clearly the nature of Israel's failure: the inability to recognize that righteousness comes from God, the attempt to establish their own kind of righteousness through observance of the Torah, and their unwillingness to accept God's way of righteousness through Jesus' death and resurrection. In 10:4 he proclaims Christ to be "the end of the Law," most likely in the sense that he is the purpose or goal toward which the Law was always pointing, since Christ brings justification to all who believe.

For Meditation: Paul here and throughout Romans is reasoning from the overwhelmingly positive experience of the gospel that he had. He had come to see Jesus Christ as the only real way to God and to right relationship with God. But Paul's own zeal may have blinded him to the genuine piety of Jews who observe the Torah simply to serve God in the way that God had revealed. The attitude that Paul attributes to Jews who pursue righteousness through observance of the Torah is often called legalism. By no means a condition peculiar to Jews, legalism is in fact manifested by many religious people. Have you experienced legalism in your own life as a Christian?

Biblical Confirmations (10:5-13)

[5] Moses writes about the righteousness that comes from the law, "The one who does these things will live by them." [6] But the righteousness that comes from faith says, "Do not say in your heart, 'Who will go up to heaven?' (that is, to bring Christ down) [7] or 'Who will go down into the abyss?' " (that is, to bring Christ up from the dead). [8] But what does it say? "The word is near you, in your mouth and in your heart" (that is, the word of faith that we preach), [9] for if you confess with your mouth that Jesus is Lord and believe in your heart that God raised him from the dead, you will be saved. [10] For one believes with the heart and so is justified, and one confesses with the mouth and so is saved. [11] For the Scripture says, "No one who believes in him will be put to shame." [12] For there is no distinction between Jew and Greek; the same Lord is Lord of all, enriching all who call upon him. [13] For "everyone who calls on the name of the Lord will be saved."

Throughout his letter to the Romans, Paul often engages in biblical interpretation to bolster his arguments about righteousness by faith and not by the Law. He reads all the Jewish Scriptures through the lens of the gospel, and makes them witnesses to Christ. In Leviticus 18:5 ("the one who does these things will live by them") Paul in 10:5 finds a text that he regards as representing the position of those who pursue righteousness by observance of the Law. Then he brings forward Deuteronomy 30:11-14 as expressing his own view of the gospel as God's saving word and righteousness by faith. The parenthetical interpretations of Deuteronomy 30:11-13 in 10:6-7 may reflect an early Christian tradition about Jesus' ascension and descent to the dead (see Eph 4:8-10; 1 Pt 3:19; 4:6). Paul's real interest, however, is in Deuteronomy 30:14 ("the word is near you"), which he equates with the gospel that he proclaims.

In 10:9-11 Paul takes up the language of Deuteronomy 30:14. With interlocking references to confessing with one's mouth (10:9a and 10:10b) and believing in one's heart (10:9b and 10:10a), he focuses on the content of the gospel ("Jesus is Lord" and "God raised him from the dead") and on the positive effects of embracing the gospel (justification and salvation). His argument is clinched by two more biblical quotations — Isaiah 28:16 (= Rom 10:11) and Joel 3:5 (= Rom 10:13) — that stress the connection between faith/confession and vindication/salvation. The intervening comment in 10:12 ("there is no distinction . . .") repeats the idea that the gospel is available ("near") to all peoples.

For Meditation: The gospel is neither hidden nor esoteric. Rather, it is accessible to all who hear it, believe it, and make it their own by confessing and living it. The gospel, and not the Mosaic Law, brings life and right relationship with God. And the Scriptures bear witness to it. The language of Romans 10:9-11 is used in some Christian circles today as teaching that belief in the gospel and confession of it guarantee one's salvation. Do you regard embracing the gospel as a once-for-all-time event, or as an ongoing process?

Accepting and Rejecting the Gospel (10:14-21)

[14] But how can they call on him in whom they have not believed? And how can they believe in him of whom they have not heard? And how can they hear without someone to preach? [15] And how can people preach unless they are sent? As it is written, "How beautiful are the feet of those who bring the good news!" [16] But not everyone has heeded the good news; for Isaiah says, "Lord, who has believed what was heard from us?" [17] This faith comes from what is heard, and what is heard comes through the word of Christ.

[18] But I ask, did they not hear? Certainly they did; for "Their voice has gone to all the earth, and their words to the ends of the world." [19] But I ask, did not Israel understand? First Moses says: "I will make you jealous of those who are not a nation; with a senseless nation I will make you angry." [20] Then Isaiah speaks boldly and says: "I was found by those who were not seeking me; I revealed myself to those who were not asking for me." [21] But regarding Israel

he says, "All day long I stretched out my hands to a disobedient and contentious people."

In describing how people come to accept the gospel, Paul in 10:14-15 works backward from calling on Christ, through believing the gospel and hearing the gospel, to God's sending those who proclaim the gospel. That preachers had been sent by God is confirmed by Isaiah 52:7 ("How beautiful are the feet of those who bring the good news"). The process is described again in 10:17 — with reference to faith based on hearing the gospel ("the word of Christ"). Since in this part of the letter Paul is explaining why not all of Israel has accepted the gospel, in 10:16 he anticipates the objection that non-Christian Israel has not been given the chance to hear the gospel. He does so by using Isaiah 53:1 to assert that the problem lay not with the proclamation and hearing of the gospel but with Israel's unwillingness to believe it.

That Israel heard and should have understood the gospel is explained in 10:18-21 with the help of four biblical quotations. That Israel heard the gospel is affirmed in 10:18 by interpreting Psalm 19(18):5 to describe the gospel ("their voice . . . their words") as spreading through the Mediterranean world ("to all the earth . . . to the ends of the world"). That Israel should have understood the gospel is established in 10:19-21 by citing the Law (Dt 32:21) and the Prophets (Is 65:1) to the effect that if Gentiles understood and accepted the gospel, how much more should Jews have done so. In 10:21 Paul concludes his biblical argument by quoting Isaiah 65:2 to trace Israel's rejection of the gospel to its own disobedience and contrariness.

For Meditation: Paul's analysis of the process of accepting the gospel — proclamation, hearing, understanding, believing, and confessing — defines what remains the mission of the Church in our world today. Although Paul used this analysis negatively to explain Jewish rejection of the gospel, it can also be taken positively as a shrewd diagnosis of how people come to embrace the gospel of Jesus Christ. If you lived in Paul's time (whether as a Jew or as a Gentile), do you think that you would have accepted the gospel?

A Remnant Within Israel (11:1-10)

¹I ask, then, has God rejected his people? Of course not! For I too am an Israelite, a descendant of Abraham, of the tribe of Benjamin. ²God has not rejected his people whom he foreknew. Do you not know what the Scripture says about Elijah, how he pleads with God against Israel? ³"Lord, they have killed your prophets, they have torn down your altars, and I alone am left, and they are seeking my life." ⁴But what is God's response to him? "I have left for myself seven thousand men who have not knelt to Baal." ⁵So also at the present time there is a remnant chosen by grace. ⁶But if by grace, it is no longer because of works; otherwise grace would no longer be grace.

⁷What then? What Israel was seeking it did not attain, but the elect attained it; the rest were hardened, ⁸as it is written: "God gave them a spirit of

deep sleep, eyes that should not see and ears that should not hear, down to this very day." [9]And David says: "Let their table become a snare and a trap, a stumbling block and a retribution for them; [10]let their eyes grow dim so that they may not see, and keep their backs bent forever."

Having explained as best he could why many in Israel had not accepted the gospel, Paul refuses to conclude that God has rejected Israel as his people. Indeed, he strongly disputes such an insinuation ("Of course not!") and takes as proof his own credentials as an Israelite (11:1-2a). Rather than denying his Jewishness, Paul views himself and other Jewish Christians as a "remnant" within Israel. To illustrate what such a remnant is, he invokes in 11:2b-4 the biblical example of the prophet Elijah and the seven thousand within Israel who alone refused to worship the Cannanite god Baal (see 1 Kgs 9:10, 14, 18). In 11:5-6 he applies the concept of the remnant to the Jewish Christians of his own time. What distinguishes them from other Jews is that God has freely chosen them and they have recognized that God deals in the realm of grace rather than in that of works of the Law.

While the Jewish Christian remnant attained what Israel sought (righteousness, see 9:31), the rest of Israel failed to do so. In 11:7 Paul describes the latter as "hardened" (see also 11:25). Then he develops the image of Israel's spiritual blindness first in 11:8 with reference to Deuteronomy 29:3 and Isaiah 29:10 ("eyes that should not see") and then in 11:9-10 by quoting Psalm 69(68):23-24 ("let their eyes grow dim"). Paul uses these precedents for God's blinding some in Israel to show the continuity between biblical times and his own day.

For Meditation: Even as a Christian, Paul never denied his Jewishness or claimed to have ceased being a Jew. Moreover, Paul could not imagine the Church as totally divorced from its Jewish roots and Christianity as an entirely separate religion. Even though many Jews did not accept the gospel, those that did served as the bridge between historic Israel and the Gentiles as members of God's people. Why do you think that Paul was so adamant about his identity as a Jew and the role of the Jewish-Christian remnant in God's plan?

Jews and Gentiles (11:11-16)

[11] Hence I ask, did they stumble so as to fall? Of course not! But through their transgression salvation has come to the Gentiles, so as to make them jealous. [12] Now if their transgression is enrichment for the world, and if their diminished number is enrichment for the Gentiles, how much more their full number.

[13] Now I am speaking to you Gentiles. Inasmuch then as I am the apostle of the Gentiles, I glory in my ministry [14] in order to make my race jealous and thus save some of them. [15] For if their rejection is the reconciliation of the world, what will their acceptance be but life from the dead? [16] If the firstfruits are holy, so is the whole batch of dough; and if the root is holy, so are the branches.

In the Jewish rejection of the gospel, Paul in 11:11-12 finds God's providence at work. Far from constituting Israel's fall, the failure of some Jews to embrace the gospel ("their transgression") was God's means of opening up the gospel to non-Jews and moving Christianity beyond the limits of ethnic Israel. This development served as "enrichment" for the world and for the Gentiles. Instead of giving up on Israel, God will use the Gentile acceptance of the gospel to make Israel jealous of those Gentiles who now enjoy membership in God's people though Christ. This will lead in turn the "full number" in Israel to accept the gospel as God's way of salvation.

These same ideas are reiterated in 11:13-15, where Paul directs his teaching to Gentile Christians who apparently needed instruction on their spiritual debt to Israel. Speaking as one whose special vocation was to be the apostle to the Gentiles (see Gal 2:7, 9), Paul in 11:14 explains his apostolic activity in terms of making Israel "jealous." In 11:15 he describes Jewish rejection of the gospel as God's way of bringing about "the reconciliation of the world" by making the gospel available to all nations. If Jewish rejection of the gospel has had such a positive effect, how much more will Jewish acceptance of the gospel bring? Indeed, it will mean the general resurrection that is part of the full coming of God's kingdom. In 11:16 the images of "firstfruits" making holy a whole batch of dough (see Nm 15:20-21) and of a "root" making holy the branches of a tree shift the focus from future to past and present, and prepare for the allegory of the olive tree.

For Meditation: Paul never gave up on Israel. Indeed, he was convinced that its partial rejection of the gospel was providential, and that the final state of God's kingdom will embrace "all Israel." He reminds Gentile Christians that their claim to holiness is rooted in Israel. The "jealousy" motif is peculiar and perhaps hard to take seriously now. And yet it was Paul's theological conclusion based on his best effort to discern God's purposes in Gentile acceptance and Jewish rejection of the gospel. Do the Jewish roots of Christian faith have a place in your spirituality?

The Olive Tree (11:17-24)

[17] But if some of the branches were broken off, and you, a wild olive shoot, were grafted in their place and have come to share in the rich root of the olive tree, [18] do not boast against the branches. If you do boast, consider that you do not support the root; the root supports you.

[19] Indeed you will say, "Branches were broken off so that I might be grafted in." [20] That is so. They were broken off because of unbelief, but you are there because of faith. So do not become haughty, but stand in awe. [21] For if God did not spare the natural branches, perhaps he will not spare you either. [22] See, then, the kindness and severity of God: severity toward those who fell, but God's kindness to you, provided you remain in his kindness; otherwise you too will be cut off.

[23] And they also, if they do not remain in unbelief, will be grafted in, for God is able to graft them in again. [24] For you were cut from what is by nature a wild olive tree, and grafted contrary to nature, into

a cultivated one, how much more will they who belong to it by nature be grafted back into their own olive tree.

To illustrate how Jewish Christians, Gentile Christians, and other Jews relate in God's plan, Paul uses the allegory of the olive tree. In an allegory each element stands for something else. The olive tree symbolizes Israel as the people of God (see Jer 11:16; Hos 14:6) now represented by Jewish Christians like Paul. Jews who reject the gospel are equated with branches broken off from the olive tree, and Gentiles who accept the gospel are equated with wild olive shoots grafted into the olive tree (11:17). From this relationship, Paul in 11:18 draws a warning to Gentile Christians not to regard themselves as separate from or superior to the Jewish people.

In 11:19-22 Paul continues the olive tree imagery and the warning to the Gentiles. Although believing Gentiles may have replaced Jews on the olive tree, the basis of their sharing in the olive tree's life is faith. And faith is not something to boast about as if it were a personal achievement (see 3:27-31). Rather, the inclusion of Gentiles is solely an act of God's kindness. So Gentile Christians should learn from God's severity to Israel and recognize that they too run the risk of being cut off.

In 11:23-24 Paul continues the olive tree imagery with particular attention to Jews who have not yet come to believe. They can become part of the olive tree again if they do not remain in unbelief. Indeed if God could make Gentiles part of the olive tree, how much more easily can God make Jews part of the olive tree once more.

For Meditation: In the course of Romans 9–11 Paul has been assembling and analyzing the various elements in God's plan. With the allegory of the olive tree he is able to demonstrate graphically how the pieces fit together. He marvels at what God has already done with Jewish Christians (continuity with Israel) and with Gentile Christians (the reconciliation of the world). He is also convinced that even Jews who reject the gospel have an essential role in God's plan. On what grounds can one be cut off from God's people?

The Mystery of Salvation (11:25-32)

25 I do not want you to be unaware of this mystery, brothers, so that you will not become wise in your own estimation: a hardening has come upon Israel in part, until the full number of the Gentiles comes in, 26 and thus all Israel will be saved, as is written: "The deliverer will come out of Zion, he will turn away godlessness from Jacob; 27 and this is my covenant with them when I take away their sins."

28 In respect to the gospel, they are enemies on your account; but in respect to election, they are beloved because of the patriarchs. 29 For the gifts and the call of God are irrevocable. 30 Just as you once disobeyed God but have now received mercy because of their disobedience, 31 so they have now disobeyed in order that, by virtue of the mercy shown to you, they too may now receive mercy. 32 For God delivered all to disobedience, that he might have mercy upon all.

Again speaking directly to Gentile Christians and warning them against illusions about their superiority, Paul in 11:25-26a states his understanding of the future unfolding of God's plan. After the partial "hardening" of Israel has allowed the full complement of Gentiles to become members of God's people, "all Israel" will be saved. The expression "all Israel" is collective, not necessarily including each and every Israelite. When this will take place is not stated, though 11:15 ("what will their acceptance be but life from the dead?") suggests that it will be part of the full coming of God's kingdom. In the light of Romans as a whole, Israel's salvation would seem to demand a direct connection with Christ, perhaps along the lines of Paul's own experience of the risen Lord. The result is expressed in 11:26b-27 with the help of quotations from Isaiah 59:20-21 ("he will turn away godlessness from Jacob") and 27:9 ("when I take away their sins").

In 11:28-29 Paul reflects on the relations between "hardened" Israel and Gentile Christians. That hardening has been providential for the Gentiles. And yet Israel remains God's "beloved," and God's gifts to Israel are "irrevocable" (see 9:4-5). Whereas Gentile Christians who were once disobedient now receive mercy from God, Jews who are now disobedient will receive mercy from God (11:30-31). Recalling 1:18–3:20, Paul concludes that "God delivered all to disobedience, that he might have mercy upon all" (11:32).

For Meditation: Despite the rejection of the gospel by many in Israel, Paul remained convinced that God's gifts to Israel and its vocation to be a light for the nations are still in force. Moreover, he was convinced that in God's merciful providence "all Israel will be saved." Although Paul is sometimes accused of anti-Judaism (see 1 Thes 2:14-16), that accusation is hard to sustain in the light of Romans 11. How might Paul's vision of God's plan serve as the basis for improved Christian-Jewish relations?

Celebratory Conclusion (11:33-36)

> [33] Oh, the depth of the riches and wisdom and knowledge of God! How inscrutable are his judgments and how unsearchable his ways! [34] "For who has known the mind of the Lord or who has been his counselor?" [35] "Or who has given him anything that he may be repaid?" [36] For from him and through him and for him are all things. To him be glory forever. Amen.

In Romans 9–11 Paul has faced difficult questions and arrived at surprising and important insights regarding God's plan for Jewish Christians, Gentile Christians, and other Jews. At last it is time to celebrate, and he does so with a hymn of praise to God. The celebration begins with two exclamations (11:33) about the wise and provident God. Then in 11:34-35 there are biblical quotations from Isaiah 40:13 and Job 41:3 that take the form of rhetorical questions and celebrate the knowledge, wisdom, and riches of God. Finally in 11:36 there is blessing of God as the origin and goal of all creation, and a final affirmation ("Amen").

For Meditation: This is a wonderful prayer on its own, and we would do well to make it our own. But Paul used it as the conclusion to his long meditation on salvation history in Romans 9–11. In what ways is this prayer an appropriate conclusion to Paul's meditation?

VII

The Gospel and Christian Life

Paul wrote as a pastoral theologian. He wanted to help his readers to understand themselves and to conduct their lives in the light of what God has done in and through Christ. In Romans 12–13 Paul provides general advice about Christian life. After offering some ways of thinking about Christian life in 12:1-8, he gives instructions about love toward others (12:9-21), attitudes toward the Roman empire (13:1-7), love as fulfilling the Law (13:8-10), and the implications of the coming Day of the Lord for Christian conduct (13:11-14).

Compared with the rest of Paul's letter to the Romans, this section is relatively easy to understand. Nevertheless, its teachings are very important, since they function as a bridge between the rich theology of chapters 1–11 and the practical advice given in the rest of the letter.

The Body of Christ and the Gifts of the Spirit (12:1-8)

[1] I urge you therefore, brothers, by the mercies of God, to offer your bodies as a living sacrifice, holy and pleasing to God, your spiritual worship. [2] Do not conform yourself to this age but be transformed by

the renewal of your mind, that you may discern what is the will of God, what is good and pleasing and perfect.

³ For by the grace given to me I tell everyone among you not to think of himself more highly than one ought to think, but to think soberly, each according to the measure of faith that God has apportioned. ⁴ For as in one body we have many parts, and all the parts do not have the same function, ⁵ so we, though many, are one body in Christ and individually parts of one another.

⁶ Since we have gifts that differ according to the grace given to us, let us exercise them: if prophecy, in proportion to the faith; ⁷ if ministry, in ministering; if one is a teacher, in teaching; ⁸ if one exhorts, in exhortation; if one contributes, in generosity; if one is over others, with diligence; if one does acts of mercy, with cheerfulness.

Before presenting general and specific advice to the Roman Christians, Paul in 12:1-8 offers some basic perspectives on Christian life: Christian life as spiritual worship (12:1-2), the body of Christ (12:3-5), and the gifts of the Holy Spirit (12:6-8).

In imparting these teachings, Paul in 12:1 adopts a hortatory stance ("I urge you") rather than giving commands. He portrays everyday Christian life in the world as an act of worship more pleasing to God than sacrifices offered in a temple. He uses cultic language ("a living sacrifice, holy and pleasing to God") in describing what he paradoxically calls "spiritual worship." Furthermore, since through Jesus' death and resurrection Christians already enjoy by way of anticipation the benefits of "the age to come," they ought to live in a manner appropriate to their identity in Christ, and so discern and follow God's will rather than conforming to "this age" (12:2).

As a way of encouraging proper humility and mutual respect within the Christian community, Paul in 12:3-5 appeals to the image of the body of Christ. The image of the human body made up of many parts and all working toward a goal (12:4) was as common in Paul's day as it is in our own ("the body politic"). By highlighting Christ's role in forming the body ("one body in Christ"), however, he gives a further theological reason why Christians should respect and defer to one another: Because it was Christ who brought them together and made them into one body.

The theme of the gifts (*charismata*) of the Holy Spirit has been anticipated in 12:3 ("by the grace given to me . . . the measure of faith"). In 12:6a Paul summarizes his teaching on a topic developed at great length in 1 Corinthians 12–14. The "charisms" are gifts from God, serve to actualize God's grace and make it concrete, differ one from another, and serve the common good. The charisms listed in 12:6b-8 are not limited to church offices or arranged in an obvious order of importance. Rather, they illustrate how the Holy Spirit's gifts might contribute to the ongoing life of the Christian community.

For Meditation: The topics in 12:1-8 — Christian life as spiritual worship, the body of Christ, and the gifts of the Holy Spirit — introduce Paul's practical advice about living out the gospel. They contain some of the most profound insights concerning Christian life in the entire Bible: to perceive Christian life as an act of continuous worship of God and to live as one already justified by faith and enjoying the benefits of God's kingdom, to see oneself as part of the one body formed by Christ, and to recognize that one's spiritual gifts are to be used for others. They provide a solid theological foundation for the ethical advice that follows. How might these insights affect your self-understanding and behavior, and your relationship with others?

Love Toward Others (12:9-21)

⁹Let love be sincere; hate what is evil, hold on to what is good; ¹⁰love one another with mutual affection; anticipate one another in showing honor. ¹¹Do not grow slack in zeal, be fervent in spirit, serve the Lord. ¹²Rejoice in hope, endure in affliction, persevere in prayer. ¹³Contribute to the needs of the holy ones, exercise hospitality.

¹⁴Bless those who persecute you, bless and do not curse them. ¹⁵Rejoice with those who rejoice, weep with those who weep. ¹⁶Have the same regard for one another; do not be haughty but associate with the lowly; do not be wise in your own estimation.

¹⁷Do not repay anyone evil for evil; be concerned for what is noble in the sight of all. ¹⁸If possible, on your part, live at peace with all. ¹⁹Beloved, do not look for revenge but leave room for wrath; for it is written, "Vengeance is mine, I will repay, says the Lord." ²⁰Rather "if your enemy is hungry, feed him; if he is thirsty, give him something to drink; for by so doing you will heap burning coals upon his head."

[21] Do not be conquered by evil but conquer evil with good.

Having laid a theological foundation for living out the gospel in everyday life, Paul in 12:9-21 presents three blocks of teaching about love toward others. The language is general and applicable to many situations. While 12:9-13 deals mainly with love toward fellow Christians, 12:14-21 concerns mainly love toward outsiders, especially one's enemies.

The advice about love within the Christian community in 12:9-13 assumes the form of short sentences that can be taken separately and in different orders. An orientation toward fellow Christians is suggested by such commands as "serve the Lord" (12:11), "persevere in prayer" (12:12), and "contribute to the needs of the holy ones" (= fellow Christians, 12:13).

The command to bless one's persecutors (12:14) seems to echo Jesus' saying in Matthew 5:44 ("love your enemies, and pray for those who persecute you"), though Paul does not refer to Jesus as the source of the saying. The other sayings in 12:15-16 could apply equally to fellow Christians or to outsiders. However, a sympathetic and modest bearing would presumably be effective in attracting outsiders to the Christian movement.

Again, the command "Do not repay anyone evil for evil" in 12:17 is reminiscent of Jesus' teaching about non-retaliation according to Matthew 5:38-42. The Christian ideal is to "live at peace with all" (12:18). But Paul was enough of a realist to know that conflicts will inevitably arise. When conflict occurs, the Christian is to leave wrath and revenge to God alone in accord with Deuteronomy 32:35 ("Vengeance is mine"). Paul then in 12:20 quotes the curious teaching of Proverbs 25:21-22 that counsels good deeds toward enemies as a way of shaming them and breaking down their hostility. In 12:21 Paul observes that evil can be overcome only by the power of good deeds issuing from love, and not by fighting evil with evil.

For Meditation: People of good will from various religious traditions can affirm much of what Paul says about love toward others in 12:9-21. But love of enemies and non-retaliation in the face of evil are distinctively Christian teaching. These teachings were best exemplified by Jesus himself. And yet it is very hard to love those who hate us and to repay evil with good. And there is no guarantee that following these teachings will disarm one's enemies and make them see the error of their ways. Have you tried to practice these teachings, and what were the results?

Christian Life in the Roman Empire (13:1-7)

¹Let every person be subordinate to the higher authorities, for there is no authority except from God, and those that exist have been established by God. ²Therefore, whoever resists authority opposes what God has appointed, and those who oppose it will bring judgment upon themselves. ³For rulers are not a cause of fear to good conduct, but to evil. Do you wish to have no fear of authority? Then do what is good and you will receive approval from it, ⁴for it

is a servant of God for your good. But if you do evil, be afraid, for it does not bear the sword without purpose; it is the servant of God to inflict wrath on the evildoer. ⁵Therefore, it is necessary to be subject not only because of the wrath but also because of conscience. ⁶This is why you also pay taxes, for the authorities are ministers of God, devoting themselves to this very thing. ⁷Pay to all their dues, taxes to whom taxes are due, toll to whom toll is due, respect to whom respect is due, honor to whom honor is due.

The spreading of the gospel throughout the Mediterranean world in the first century was facilitated to a large extent by the Roman empire, especially by the relative peacefulness that it imposed and by the opportunities for travel by land and sea that it provided. Rome was the capital of the empire. And the Christians at Rome were probably already under some official scrutiny. This perhaps helps to explain why Paul's advice to them regarding their attitude toward the Roman empire is quite irenic and cooperative. Much in 13:1-7 echoes the sentiments of other Jewish writers (Ben Sira, Josephus) and is echoed by other early Christian texts (see Mk 12:13-17; 1 Tm 2:1-2; Ti 3:1; 1 Pt 2:13-17). For a very different view of the Roman empire, however, see the book of Revelation, which speaks to the experiences of Christians in Asia Minor in the late first century who were being forced to participate in emperor worship and other civic religious rites.

In 13:1-7 Paul counsels the Roman Christians to cooperate with the imperial officials and the empire as a whole. The language of 13:1a ("be subordinate to the higher authorities") presupposes a society in which status and good order are important values. Paul gives several reasons for cooperation: The officials' authority is from God (13:1b); they carry out what God intends (13:2); and they are God's instruments both to reward and to punish (13:3-4). Those who act properly have nothing to fear from the Roman officials, whereas evildoers have good reason to fear them. Thus cooperation with the Roman officials is both prudent ("because of the wrath") and the right thing for Christians to do ("because of conscience," 13:5). In light of these principles, Paul in 13:6-7 urges the Roman Christians to pay the taxes incumbent upon them, and to respect and honor the government officials.

For Meditation: This text has often been misused by evil governments to oppress their people. Also, it has sometimes been taken as the basis for the Christian doctrine of Church and state. In fact, it is best understood as Paul's practical advice to the very small Christian community at Rome in the middle of the first century A.D. That this community could directly change or even influence the social and political structures of the Roman empire was very unlikely. Moreover, Paul and other early Christians probably did not expect the Roman empire to last long (see 13:11-12a). How Paul's advice looks to Christians today depends greatly on their own social and political context. Where Christians form a tiny minority and the local government is basically just, Romans 13:1-7 may be sound advice. But where the local government is unjust, one may find better advice in Revelation. Where Christians constitute a majority, Paul's stance can seem too passive and runs the risk of allowing the state to coopt the Church. How does Paul's advice look to you in your social context?

The Love Command and the Day of the Lord (13:8-14)

8 Owe nothing to anyone, except to love one another; for the one who loves another has fulfilled the law. 9 The commandments, "You shall not commit adultery; you shall not kill; you shall not steal; you shall not covet," and whatever other commandments there may be, are summed up in this saying, namely "You shall love your neighbor as yourself." 10 Love does no evil to the neighbor; hence, love is the fulfillment of the law.

11 And do this because you know the time; it is the hour now for you to awake from sleep. For our salvation is nearer now than when we first believed; 12 the night is advanced, the day is at hand. Let us throw off the works of darkness and put on the armor of light; 13 let us conduct ourselves properly as in the day, not in orgies and drunkenness, not in promiscuity and licentiousness, not in rivalry and jealousy. 14 But put on the Lord Jesus Christ, and make no provision for the desires of the flesh.

Having advised the Roman Christians to pay their taxes, Paul in 13:8-10 continues the financial imagery ("owe nothing to anyone") but returns to the theme of love toward others (see 12:9-21). The claim that "one who loves another has fulfilled the law" (13:8; see also Gal 5:14) is explained with reference to the biblical prohibitions against adultery, killing, stealing, and coveting (see Ex 20:13-17; Dt 5:17-21). One who truly loves others will never transgress these commandments. The idea is given further biblical basis in 13:9 by the quotation of Leviticus 19:18 ("you shall love your neighbor as yourself") — a text frequently cited in the New Testament as a summary of the Torah (see Mt 5:43; 19:19; 22:39; Mk 12:31, 33; Lk 10:27; Gal 5:14; Jas 2:8). Since love does no evil to the other and since the goal of the Law is to prevent evildoing, love can be described as the fulfillment of the Law.

In 13:11-14 Paul concludes his general advice by introducing the idea of the imminent coming of God's kingdom and the stance of vigilance in conduct that it demands. In 13:11-12a he reminds his readers of the nearness of the Day of the Lord in various ways, and observes that for the faithful that Day will bring "salvation." Then in 13:12b-14 he insists that the coming Day of the Lord demands appropriate behavior by way of preparation. Using the common images of day/night and light/darkness, Paul calls his readers to "put on the armor of light" (13:12; see Eph 6:11-17 for a fuller development of the imagery). This means the same as to "put on the Lord Jesus Christ" (13:14) and living by the spirit rather than by the flesh.

For Meditation: This text stresses two guiding principles of Christian life: love as the fulfillment of the Law, and appropriate conduct as preparation for the full coming of God's kingdom. Far from being unique to Paul, they appear on practically every page in the New Testament. But they are often far from our consciousness today. Do these principles have a direct influence on what you do and what you do not do?

VIII
The Gospel and Community Conflict

Whereas Paul's advice in Romans 12–13 is general, in 14:1–15:13 he is clearly addressing a concrete pastoral problem that was dividing Christians at Rome. The precise nature of the problem remains elusive to us. The factions are called the "strong" and the "weak." While the "weak" hesitate to eat certain foods (see 14:2) and wish to observe certain days (see 14:5), the "strong" insist that "nothing is unclean in itself" (14:14). Whatever the precise issues were, Paul regarded them as matters of "opinions" (14:1) and as not essential to Christian faith (see 14:5). His concluding appeal to Christ as the one who unifies Jews and Gentiles (15:7-13) suggests a division along ethnic lines. But his dismissal of the controversy as mere "opinions" indicates that something less serious than the basic separation of Jews and Gentiles before and apart from Christ was at issue.

How much Paul himself knew about the nature of the community conflict at Rome is also not clear. Paul had not yet visited Rome (see 1:13), and so he had to rely on the reports of others. However, as chapter 16 shows, Paul had access to a wide network of communication with the Christian community at Rome. This in turn raises the question of how important Romans 14:1–15:13 is in the letter as a whole. Some view it as the climax to which everything in Romans 1–13 had been moving. Others see it as a practical application of Paul's theological insights to a minor pastoral problem at Rome.

The passage is especially important as an illustration of Paul's skill as a pastoral theologian. Unlike the case of the incestuous man at Corinth (see 1 Cor 5:1-5) where Paul's response is vigorous and unyielding, here as in 1 Corinthians 8–10 (the case of eating meat sacrificed to idols) Paul regards the matter of the dispute to be morally and religiously indifferent but the fact of the dispute as very significant and dangerous to the Christian community.

In giving advice to those in the conflict, Paul urges them to avoid condemning others (14:1-12) and to respect the consciences of others (14:13-23). He appeals to the self-sacrificing love of Christ (15:1-6), who has united Jews and Gentiles in the one body of Christ (15:7-13). Even though on the intellectual level Paul agrees with the "strong," in his pastoral advice he takes the part of the "weak" and calls on the "strong" to respect the sensitivities of the "weak."

Community conflict is part of human life and so of spirituality. Paul's letters show that community conflict was part of Christian life from earliest times. To observe Paul's pastoral strategy and to meditate on its theological foundations can help Christians today to deal with the conflicts that we inevitably experience in our families, churches, cities, and nations.

Avoid Condemning Others (14:1-12)

[1] Welcome anyone who is weak in faith, but not for disputes over opinions. [2] One person believes that one may eat anything, while the weak person eats only vegetables. [3] The one who eats must not despise the one who abstains, and the one who abstains must not pass judgment on the one who eats; for God has welcomed him. [4] Who are you to pass judgment on someone else's servant? Before his own master he stands or falls. And he will be upheld, for the Lord is able to make him stand.

[5] For one person considers one day more important than another, while another person considers all alike. Let everyone be fully persuaded in his own mind. [6] Whoever observes the day, observes it for the Lord. Also whoever eats, eats for the Lord, since he gives thanks to God; while whoever abstains, abstains for the Lord and gives thanks to God.

[7] None of us lives for oneself, and no one dies for oneself. [8] For if we live, we live for the Lord, and if we die, we die for the Lord; so then, whether we live or die, we are the Lord's. [9] For this is why Christ died and came to life, that he might be Lord of both the dead and the living. [10] Why then do you judge your brother? Or you, why do you look down on your brother? For we shall all stand before the judgment seat of God; [11] for it is written: "As I live, says the Lord, every knee shall bend before me, and every tongue shall give praise to God." [12] So then each of us shall give an account of himself to God.

With his opening comment in 14:1 Paul makes clear that he is addressing the "strong" at Rome (even though the "weak" appear to be causing the problem) and urges them to accept as fellow Christians those who hold different views. Moreover, he indicates that he does not regard the issues at dispute to be of vital importance but merely "opinions." According to 14:2 one aspect of the dispute concerned what foods may be eaten. Whereas the "strong" eat anything, the "weak" eat only vegetables. No Jewish group in antiquity was known to promote vegetarianism. It could be, however, that Jewish Christians, still respectful of the Jewish food laws, felt safe at mixed gatherings by restricting themselves to eating vegetables (see Dn 1). Since Paul did not consider whatever was the precise problem an important issue, his major concern was that neither group condemn the other. The reason is that God had accepted both into the community of faith. Whomever God has accepted, no human has the right to condemn (14:3). Then in 14:4 he uses the analogy of the master and a servant (probably a slave). No human master can legitimately pass judgment on a servant belonging to another master. But all Christians are servants of God and have the one God as their only real Master. Therefore, Christians have no right to judge one another, since they would be usurping the prerogative of God, the master and judge of all.

According to 14:5-6, a second issue in the dispute concerned the observance of certain days as sacred or at least of special importance. Again it is hard to be precise about the point of the dispute. Jews, of course, had a rather full sacred calendar, and so the reference could be to Sabbaths and Holy Days (Passover, Pentecost, New Year, Day of Atonement, Tabernacles, etc.). But the reference could also be to fast days

(Jewish or not) or even to favorable days according to astrologers. Again, Paul's concern is not with the observance itself but with how one behaves, with whether one seeks only to honor and thank God.

In 14:7-9 Paul develops the theme of belonging to the Lord. Those who are "in Christ" no longer live or die for themselves alone (14:7). Rather, in both life and death they now belong to the Lord, who is the Lord of both the dead and the living (14:8-9). From this basic truth of Christian faith, Paul returns in 14:10-12 to the specific issue of passing judgment on fellow Christians. Condemning fellow Christians is wrong because it takes over what is rightfully the task of God and fails to discern the radical equality that exists among Christians in the present and in the future: "For we shall all stand before the judgment seat of God" (14:10). The point is confirmed with a biblical quotation from Isaiah 49:18/45:23 in 14:11, to the effect that all of us will stand before God as our judge.

For Meditation: The enthusiasm of one group (the "weak") in the community at Rome for avoiding certain foods and for observing certain days had led to serious conflicts between Christians. Paul considered the issues to be matters of indifference. But he was not indifferent to the reactions that the dispute had provoked. And so he urged both parties to respect their dignity and equality as Christians based upon their belonging to the Lord. He also appealed to their belief in God as their ultimate master and judge. If we recognize that in the last judgment we will all stand before God, we will be slow to pass judgment on others. Would Paul's approach help you in dealing with a dispute in your family, community, church, school, or other group?

Respect for the Conscience of Others (14:13-23)

[13] Then let us no longer judge one another, but rather resolve never to put a stumbling block or hindrance in the way of a brother. [14] I know and am convinced in the Lord that nothing is unclean in itself; still, it is unclean for someone who thinks it unclean. [15] If your brother is being hurt by what you eat, your conduct is no longer in accord with love. Do not because of your food destroy him for whom Christ died. [16] So do not let your good be reviled. [17] For the kingdom of God is not a matter of food and drink, but of righteousness, peace, and joy in the Holy Spirit; [18] whoever serves Christ in this way is pleasing to God and approved by others.

[19] Let us then pursue what leads to peace and to building up one another. [20] For the sake of food, do not destroy the work of God. Everything is indeed clean, but it is wrong for anyone to become a stumbling block by eating; [21] it is good not to eat meat or drink wine or do anything that causes your brother to stumble. [22] Keep the faith that you have to yourself in the presence of God; blessed is the one who does not condemn himself for what he approves. [23] But whoever has doubts is condemned if he eats, because this is not from faith; for whatever is not from faith is sin.

In 14:13-18 Paul continues to address the "strong." Instead of condemning the "weak," the "strong" should be careful not to put any obstacle (*skandalon*) in the way of another's faith (15:13). Paul agrees with their principle that "nothing is unclean in itself" (15:14; see also 1 Cor 10:25-27; 1 Tm 4:4; Mk 7:15, 19; Acts 10:15). But he also recognizes that some Christians may have a tender conscience on matters of food and special days (15:14b). Those with the "strong" conscience should defer to the "weak," lest food become the occasion for risking the salvation of those for whom Christ died (15:15). While the strong might appeal to their principle, Paul appeals to the even higher principle of the kingdom of God (a term that Paul rarely uses). The kingdom of God is primarily concerned with righteousness, peace, and joy in the Holy Spirit, as Romans 1–13 has shown. The matters that seem to be disturbing the Roman Christian community are not on the same level of importance (14:16-18).

The same points are made again in 14:19-23. The Christian ideal is peace and mutual edification (14:19). Even though the strong are correct in principle ("everything is indeed clean"), they have no right to stand in the way of the spiritual progress of others (14:20-21). They do have the obligation, however, to respect the conscience of others. If others truly believe that eating meat is wrong for them, and if they are forced to act against their conscience, they sin, "for whatever is not from faith is sin" (14:22-23).

For Meditation: Paul is well known as a person of principle. And yet here in a matter that he considered morally and religiously indifferent, Paul was willing to back away from his principle to accommodate the sensitivities of others, and to promote peace within the Christian community. Here the principle (with which Paul agreed) must yield to the avoidance of "scandal" (which means putting an obstacle in the way of another's faith) and to respecting the conscience of others. How do you judge Paul's advice — as pastorally sensitive, confused, or hypocritical?

The Example of Christ (15:1-6)

> [1]We who are strong ought to put up with the failing of the weak and not to please ourselves; [2]let each of us please our neighbor for the good, for building up. [3]For Christ did not please himself; but, as it is written, "The insults of those who insult you fall upon me." [4]For whatever was written previously was written for our instruction, that by endurance and by the encouragement of the Scriptures we might have hope. [5]May the God of endurance and encouragement grant you to think in harmony with one another, in keeping with Christ Jesus, [6]that with one accord you may with one voice glorify the God and Father of our Lord Jesus Christ.

In 15:1-2 ("we") Paul explicitly allies himself with the "strong" but admonishes them that the goal of Christian life is not personal development and self-gratification but rather contributing to the development and progress of others. His term is "building up" or edification, and in 15:3-4 he roots the concept in the example of Jesus' sacrificial death on our behalf.

135

In Psalm 69:10 ("the insults of those who insult you fall upon me") the word "you" refers to God. Paul interprets "me" as a reference to Christ. In 15:4 he explains why he interprets the Old Testament text in the light of Christ's passion and death. It was written for "our instruction" and "encouragement." In 15:5-6 Paul puts his pastoral advice in the form of a prayer. He asks that God may lead the Roman Christians "to think in harmony with one another" so that they may "with one voice" glorify God.

For Meditation: Thus far in dealing with the community conflict at Rome, Paul has cautioned against condemning others, urged respect for the consciences of others and recognition of the goal of building up fellow Christians, and appealed to the self-sacrificing example of Christ. To people in our day with their insistence on individual rights, personal development, and rejection of self-sacrifice as an ideal, this advice may sound peculiar and even absurd. And yet it flows out of the gospel that Paul proclaimed. Could the members of your community (family, church group, parish, school, etc.) understand and appreciate Paul's pastoral counsel?

Christ as the Principle of Unity (15:7-13)

⁷Welcome one another, then, as Christ welcomed you, for the glory of God. ⁸For I say that Christ became a minister of the circumcised to show God's truthfulness, to confirm the promises to the patriarchs, ⁹but so that the Gentiles might glorify God

for his mercy. As it is written: "Therefore, I will praise you among the Gentiles and sing praises to your name." [10]And again it says: "Rejoice, O Gentiles, with his people." [11]And again: "Praise the Lord, all you Gentiles, and let all the peoples praise him." [12]And again Isaiah says: "The root of Jesse shall come, raised up to rule the Gentiles; in him shall the Gentiles hope." [13]May the God of hope fill you with all joy and peace in believing, so that you may abound in hope by the power of the Holy Spirit.

The ultimate reason to work for harmony and mutual edification within the Christian community is based on what God has done in bringing together Jews and Gentiles. Since Christ has made all welcome in God's sight, so Christians should welcome one another (15:7). Although the ministry of the earthly Jesus as Israel's Messiah was limited to Jews ("the circumcised") in accord with God's promises to Israel, the consequence of his death and resurrection has been to open up the benefits of God's kingdom to non-Jews also. That Gentiles were intended to be part of God's people is confirmed by a collection of four Old Testament quotations that feature the term "Gentiles": Psalm 18(17):50/2 Samuel 22:50 (= Rom 15:9), Deuteronomy 32:43 (= 15:10), Psalm 116:1 (= 15:11), and Isaiah 11:10 (= 15:12). Again Paul rounds off his instruction with a prayer that God will fill the Roman Christians with joy, peace, and hope.

For Meditation: The fact that Paul appeals to the Jewish-Gentile division suggests some connection with the weak-strong conflict at Rome. The assumption seems to be that if God could unite Jews and Gentiles in Christ (thus resolving a major conflict), how much more can God unite the weak and the strong at Rome (in their conflict over "opinions"). How can the appeal to the saving work of Christ promote unity among Christians today?

IX

The Promotion of the Gospel

The final section of Romans is often skipped or skimmed. However, it too is significant for understanding the gospel according to Paul and the nature of Christian spirituality. Romans 15:14–16:27 puts us in touch with some of the ways in which the gospel was promoted in earliest Christianity and can be promoted today. Paul the apostle, of course, was an important vehicle, since he founded many churches in the Mediterranean world (15:14-33). But in his mission Paul needed and relied on the help of co-workers and other Christians — male and female, rich and poor, and Jews and Gentiles (16:1-16, 21-23). And the spiritual legacy that Paul left was taken up and applied by later generations of Christians (16:17-20, 25-27).

Apostle to the Gentiles (15:14-21)

¹⁴I myself am convinced about you, my brothers, that you yourselves are full of goodness, filled with all knowledge, and able to admonish one another. ¹⁵But I have written to remind you, because of the grace given me by God, ¹⁶to be a minister of Christ Jesus to the Gentiles in performing the priestly service of the gospel of God, so that the offering up

of the Gentiles may be acceptable, sanctified by the Holy Spirit.

[17] In Christ Jesus, then, I have reason to boast in what pertains to God. [18] For I will not dare to speak of anything except what Christ has accomplished through me to lead the Gentiles to obedience by word and deed, [19] by the power of signs and wonders, by the power of the Spirit of God, so that from Jerusalem all the way around to Illyricum, I have finished preaching the gospel of Christ.

[20] Thus I aspire to proclaim the gospel not where Christ has already been named, so that I do not build on another's foundation, [21] but as it is written: "Those who have never been told of him shall see, and those who have never heard of him shall understand."

As Paul draws his long letter to a close, and especially after his advice about the community conflict in 14:1–15:13, he seeks in 15:14 to render the Roman Christians benevolent again by praising their goodness, knowledge, and ability to solve their own problems. Also, to explain why he has written to them "rather boldly" he appeals in 15:15 to the special grace or charism given to him by God to be the apostle to the Gentiles. His letter to the Romans is really an extension of his apostolic ministry. Using the analogy of a priest who offers sacrifice to God, Paul in 15:16b portrays himself as the priest of Jesus Christ bringing the Gentiles to God as a gift or offering.

As the loyal servant of the gospel Paul has reason to boast (15:17). But the basis of all his boasting is "what Christ has accomplished through me" (15:18). In describing his ministry as empowered by the Holy Spirit, he defines in 15:19 the geographical limits of his apostolic mission thus far as from Jerusalem to Illyricum (the Roman province on the eastern coast of the Adriatic Sea).

Finally in 15:20-21 he states his guiding principle as an apostle: "to proclaim the gospel not where Christ has already been named." Paul was a founder of churches. In 15:21 he cites Isaiah 52:15 as the biblical justification for his ministry of proclaiming the gospel to the Gentiles ("those who have never been told of him"), thus fulfilling the mission of God's Servant.

For Meditation: The gospel was spread by apostles like Paul. In light of his call to bring the gospel to non-Jews, Paul wanted to found churches all over the Mediterranean world. He was primarily a pastoral theologian, not a writer or a theology professor. Indeed, his letters were written as substitutes for his personal presence. Having worked through most of Romans, how do you regard Paul? What do you like or admire? What do you find difficult or unattractive about him?

Travel Plans (15:22-33)

[22] That is why I have so often been prevented from coming to you. [23] But now, since I no longer have any opportunity in these regions and since I have desired to come to you for many years, [24] I hope to see you in passing as I go to Spain and to be sent on

my way there by you, after I have enjoyed being with you for a time.

²⁵ Now, however, I am going to Jerusalem to minister to the holy ones. ²⁶ For Macedonia and Achaia have decided to make some contribution for the poor among the holy ones in Jerusalem; ²⁷ they decided to do it, and in fact they are indebted to them, for if the Gentiles have come to share in their spiritual blessings, they ought also to serve them in material blessings. ²⁸ So when I have completed this and safely handed over this contribution to them, I shall set out by way of you to Spain; ²⁹ and I know that in coming to you I shall come in the fullness of Christ's blessing.

³⁰ I urge you, brothers, by our Lord Jesus Christ and by the love of the Spirit, to join me in the struggle by your prayers to God on my behalf, ³¹ that I may be delivered from the disobedient in Judea, and that my ministry may be acceptable to the holy ones, ³² so that I may come to you with joy by the will of God and be refreshed together with you. ³³ The God of peace be with all of you. Amen.

While in 1:13 it was not clear why Paul had not yet visited Rome, in 15:22 he implies that he was too busy founding new communities to go to a city like Rome where a Christian community was already well established. Then in 15:23-24 he states that he had done all that he could do from Jerusalem to Illyricum and announces plans for a new missionary undertaking in Spain. And so he intends to use his stay at Rome mainly as a stopping point on the way to Spain.

Before Paul could come to Rome and Spain, however, he needed to bring the proceeds of the collection that he had taken up for the "holy ones" of the Jerusalem community (see 1 Cor 16:1-4; 2 Cor 8–9). Paul intended the collection not only to alleviate the poverty of the Jerusalem Christians but also to serve as a symbolic expression of thanksgiving on the part of Gentile Christians for sharing in God's spiritual blessings upon Israel (15:25-27). Paul was confident that after the successful completion of his mission to Jerusalem, he would be able to visit Rome on his way to Spain (15:28-29).

And yet in 15:30-33 Paul suggests that his journey to Jerusalem may involve some "struggle." He fears opposition from Jews in Judea (see 1 Thes 2:14-16) and is probably not sure how his offering and his gospel will be received by the leaders of the Jewish Christian community in Jerusalem. And so he asks the prayers of the Roman Christians that his journey might be successful.

For Meditation: Paul the apostle undertook difficult journeys (see 2 Cor 11:25-28) to promote the gospel. He used the device of a collection both to alleviate the sufferings of Christians in Jerusalem and to express symbolically the unity of Jews and Gentiles in Christ. The gospel was spread primarily by people interacting with other people. When Paul did finally reach Rome, he did so as a prisoner (see Acts 25–28) rather than as a visiting apostle. What might today's Church learn from Paul's apostolic activity, and what different strategies might it need to follow?

Final Greetings (16:1-16, 21-23)

¹I commend to you Phoebe our sister, who is also a minister of the church at Cenchreae, ²that you may receive her in the Lord in a manner worthy of the holy ones and help her in whatever she may need from you, for she has been a benefactor to many and to me as well.

³Greet Prisca and Aquila, my co-workers in Christ Jesus, ⁴who risked their necks for my life, to whom not only I am grateful but also all the churches of the Gentiles; ⁵greet also the church at their house. Greet my beloved Epaenetus, who was the firstfruits in Asia for Christ. ⁶Greet Mary, who has worked hard for you. ⁷Greet Andronicus and Junia, my relatives and my fellow prisoners; they are prominent among the apostles and they were in Christ before me. ⁸Greet Ampliatus, my beloved in the Lord. ⁹Greet Urbanus, our co-worker in Christ, and my beloved Stachys. ¹⁰Greet Apelles, who is approved in Christ. Greet those who belong to the family of Aristobulus. ¹¹Greet my relative Herodion. Greet those in the Lord who belong to the family of Narcissus. ¹²Greet those workers in the Lord, Tryphaena and Tryphosa. Greet the beloved Persis, who has worked hard in the Lord. ¹³Greet Rufus, chosen in the Lord, and his mother and mine. ¹⁴Greet Asyncritus, Phlegon, Hermes, Patrobas, Hermas, and the brothers who are with them. ¹⁵Greet Philologus, Julia, Nereus and his sister, and Olympas, and all the holy ones who are with them. ¹⁶Greet one another with a holy kiss. All the churches of Christ greet you.

²¹Timothy, my co-worker, greets you; so do Lucius and Jason and Sosipater, my relatives. ²²I, Tertius, the writer of this letter, greet you in the

Lord. [23] Gaius, who is host to me and to the whole church, greets you. Erastus, the city treasurer, and our brother Quartus greet you.

Although there is some disagreement whether the greetings in Romans 16 were part of the original letter, they most likely were. In 16:1-2 Paul commends Phoebe and urges that she be accepted and granted hospitality by the Roman Christians. She is called a "minister" (*diakonos* = deacon) of the church at Cenchreae (the port of Corinth) as well as Paul's benefactor or patron (*prostatis*). She may have even been carrying Paul's letter to Rome from Corinth.

The persons listed in 16:3-16 were presumably members of the Roman Christian community. The list tells us some important things about early Christian life. The community met at the house of members who had facilities large enough to accommodate a gathering of some forty or fifty persons — in the case of Rome, at the house of Prisca and Aquila (16:3-5a; see Acts 18:1-2). Paul designates many persons in the list as "relatives" (fellow Jews), whereas others bear Gentile names, thus indicating the mixed character of the Christian community at Rome. Many names are clearly feminine (Prisca, Mary, Junia, Tryphaena and Tryphosa, etc.), indicating the prominence of women in the Roman church. It is likely that Junia is called an "apostle" (see 16:7). Many men and women are designated as Paul's co-workers (see 16:3, 9, 12), showing that Paul relied upon the collaboration of other Christians in his ministry. The symbol of the "holy kiss" (an embrace and peck on the cheek) signifies the mutual

145

respect and unity that Paul hopes will prevail in the church at Rome.

The greetings from Christians at Corinth in 16:21-23 provide further information about early Christian life. In 16:21 Timothy is called a "co-worker" and three others are designated as "relatives" (Jews). In 16:22 Tertius, the scribe responsible for writing down the letter, steps out of his role and inserts his personal greeting. From 16:23 we learn that Paul enjoys the hospitality of Gaius (presumably as man of means) and that Erastus the city treasurer of Corinth was a member of the church there.

For Meditation: The greetings to Christians in Rome from Christians in Corinth is a precious document. It shows how early Christians formed a network of communication. It shows that ethnic, social, and gender differences were transcended (see Gal 3:28) through the gospel. It shows that Paul's ministry enlisted the cooperation and support of many Christians. What can the Church today learn from Romans 16?

A Warning (16:17-20) and a Doxology (16:25-27)

[[17]I urge you, brothers, to watch out for those who create dissensions and obstacles, in opposition to the teaching that you learned; avoid them. [18]For such people do not serve our Lord Christ but their own appetites, and by fair and flattering speech they deceive the hearts of the innocent. [19]For while your obedience is known to all, so that I rejoice over you, I want you to be wise as to what is good, and simple

146

as to what is evil; [20]then the God of peace will quickly crush Satan under your feet. The grace of our Lord Jesus be with you.]

[[25]Now to him who can strengthen you, according to my gospel and the proclamation of Jesus Christ, according to the revelation of the mystery kept secret for long ages [26]but now manifested through the prophetic writings and, according to the command of the eternal God, made known to all nations to bring about the obedience of faith, [27]to the only wise God, through Jesus Christ be glory forever and ever. Amen.]

These two texts, though well represented in the manuscript tradition, were probably not originally part of Paul's letter to the Romans. Even the English translation cannot disguise the difference in vocabulary and style from the other parts of the letter.

The warning (16:17-20) may have come from a later admirer of Paul or even in another context from Paul himself. It uses language not previously found in Romans (most obviously, "Satan"), and in it Paul speaks about opponents not previously mentioned and speaks in an authoritative tone not adopted elsewhere in Romans.

The concluding doxology (16:25-27) uses some language that is prominent elsewhere in Romans ("gospel," "obedience of faith") as well as some phrases that are foreign to it ("the revelation of the mystery kept secret"). Although in some respects it is a good summary of Romans, the doxology may be from a second-century admirer of Paul.

For Meditation: These non- or post-Pauline texts illustrate how Paul's work of proclaiming the gospel was carried on by others after his death. They bear witness to the early phases in the transmission of the Pauline tradition whose beneficiaries we are today. While remaining faithful to Paul's insights and language, the tradition adapts and applies them to new situations. How do you understand the nature and role of tradition?

For Further Study

Commentaries

Byrne, B. *Romans* (Collegeville: Liturgical Press, 1996).
Cranfield, C. E. B. *A Critical and Exegetical Commmentary on the Epistle to the Romans* (Edinburgh: T & T Clark, 1975, 1979).
Dunn, J. D. G. *Romans* (Dallas: Word, 1988).
Fitzmyer, J. A. *Romans* (New York: Doubleday, 1993).
Käsemann, E. *Commentary on Romans* (Grand Rapids: Eerdmans, 1980).

Other Books

Beker, J. C. *Paul's Apocalyptic Gospel. The Coming Triumph of God* (Philadelphia: Fortress, 1982).
Donfried, K. P. (ed.). *The Romans Debate* (rev. ed.; Peabody, MA: Hendrickson, 1991).
Elliott, N. *Liberating Paul. The Justice of God and the Politics of the Apostle* (Maryknoll: Orbis, 1994).
Fitzmyer, J. A. *Spiritual Exercises Based on Paul's Epistle to the Romans* (New York: Paulist, 1995).
Gaston, L. *Paul and the Torah* (Vancouver: University of British Columbia, 1987).
Kaylor, R. D. *Paul's Covenant: Jew and Gentile in Romans* (Atlanta: Knox 1988).
Martin, B. L. *Christ and the Law in Paul* (Leiden: Brill 1989).
Räisänen, H. *Paul and the Law* (rev. ed.; Tübingen: Mohr-Siebeck, 1987).
Sanders, E. P. *Paul and Palestinian Judaism* (Philadelphia: Fortress, 1977).
_____. *Paul, the Law, and the Jewish People* (Philadelphia: Fortress, 1985).
Segal, A. F. *Paul the Convert. The Apostolate and Apostasy of Saul the Pharisee* (New Haven–London: Yale University Press, 1990).
Stowers, S. K. *A Rereading of Romans: Justice, Jews & Gentiles* (New Haven: Yale University Press, 1994).
Thielman, F. *From Plight to Solution. A Jewish Framework for Understanding Paul's View of the Law in Galatians and Romans* (Leiden: Brill, 1989).

149

Watson, F. *Paul, Judaism, and the Gentiles. A Sociological Approach* (Cambridge: Cambridge University Press, 1986).

Wedderburn, A. J. *The Reasons for Romans* (Edinburgh: T & T Clark, 1988).

Westerholm, S. *Israel's Law and the Church's Faith. Paul and His Recent Interpreters* (Grand Rapids: Eerdmans, 1988).

Wright, N. T. *The Climax of the Covenant: Christ and the Law in Pauline Theology* (Edinburgh: T & T Clark, 1991).

Bibliographies (on individual passages and other general matters)

G. Wagner (ed.). *An Exegetical Bibliography of the New Testament, vol. 4, Romans and Galatians* (Mercer, GA: Mercer University Press, 1996).

IN THE SAME SERIES FROM NEW CITY PRESS

PAUL'S PRISON LETTERS
Scriptural Commentaries on Paul's Letters to Philemon, the Philippians, and the Colossians
DANIEL HARRINGTON

"I heartily recommend this work both for the person seeking an initial familiarity with Saint Paul, and for the more advanced student eager to link exegesis with classical Ignatian spirituality. This work enhances knowledge with imaginative meditation and prayer. Once again, Father Harrington's treatment and approach is superb." (Bishop Richard Sklba)

ISBN 1-56548-088-0, paper, 5 3/8 x 8 1/2, 144 pp., $9.95

DANIEL
A book for Troubling Times
ALEXANDER A. DI LELLA

"The 'troubled times' of the title matches this century as well as the past—we are confronted by a timeless biblical work with a timely biblical commentary." (Roland E. Murphy, O. Carm.)

ISBN 1-56548-087-2, paper, 5 3/8 x 8 1/2, 160 pp., $11.95

SONG OF SONGS
The Love Poetry of Scripture
DIANNE BERGANT

Bergant's spiritual commentary is a delightfully intriguing literal reading of the Song of Songs. She develops and vividly explains the poetic elements of the sacred text and masterfully applies them to contemporary spirituality.

ISBN 1-56548-100-3, paper, 5 3/8 x 8 1/2, 152 pp., $9.95

TO ORDER PHONE 1-800-462-5980

ALSO AVAILABLE FROM NEW CITY PRESS

HOW TO READ THE GOSPELS
Answers to Common Questions
DANIEL HARRINGTON

"Here is another masterpiece from the pen of Jesuit biblical scholar Daniel Harrington ...The amount of information compressed in these few pages strongly recommends this book for group study." (Modern Liturgy)

"This is an excellent introduction. Fr. Harrington wears his vast learning lightly and writes with his characteristic clarity about the key issues in Gospel interpretation today." (Robert J. Karris, O.F.M.)

"It is a handy reference work for the religious educator." (Liguorian)

ISBN 1-56548-076-7, paper, 5 1/8 x 8, 96 pp., $6.95

THE TENDER FAREWELL OF JESUS
Meditations on Chapter 17 of John's Gospel
ADRIAN VAN KAAM; Foreword by Susan Muto

"Fr. Adrian van Kaam has written many texts and poems in his distinguished career, but this one is especially tender and touches my heart." (Mary Ellen Drushal, Ph.D.)

ISBN 1-56548-080-5, paper, 5 3/8 x 8 1/2, 128 pp., $8.95

CALL TO THE CENTER
The Gospel's Invitation to Deeper Prayer
M. BASIL PENNINGTON

"Fr. Basil leads the reader in a very personal way to listen to the Word of God in the Gospel of Matthew. His meditations show us how to open ourselves to God who gives us love, peace and joy and how to share these gifts with others in our troubled world." (Morton Kelsey)

ISBN 1-56548-070-8, paper, 5 3/8 x 8 1/2, 168 pp., $9.95

TO ORDER PHONE 1-800-462-5980